PLANNING YOUR LIFE GOD'S WAY

Practical Help from the Bible for Making Decisions

TIMOTHY W. BERREY

About *Planning Your Life God's Way*

"*Planning Your Life God's Way* renewed our devotion to know the ways of God in a personal, practical way. This refreshing material overcomes mechanical aspects of the 'traditional' approach, while affirming the individual will of God. You will appreciate biblical insights throughout and a timely emphasis on responsible obedience to Scripture."
Thomas Overmiller, Pastor, Faith Baptist Church (Queens, New York)

"Every Christian that is serious about exalting Jesus Christ is committed to knowing and doing God's will. *Planning Your Life God's Way* points believers to the timeless truths in the Bible that prepares him to do God's will in life's major decisions, as well as in the everyday mundane tasks. This is a must-read for any Christian who is passionate about glorifying God with their life."
Robbie Asuncion, Pastor, Lighthouse Bible Believers Church (Parañaque, Philippines)

"When Dr. Berrey presented this material at our church, he offered clear, God-centered and Bible-focused instruction on pursuing God's will that was helpful to any earnest follower of Christ."
Thad Berrey, Pastor, Calvary Baptist Church (Hampton, Georgia)

"As I studied the material in Dr. Berrey's book, I was helped in doing God's will for my life, even though I have been studying God's Word and seeking to follow God's will for the past 40 years. Every believer would be helped by this book. It is full of practical wisdom formed by biblical truth regarding one of life's most essential issues: discerning and doing God's will."
Phil Kamibayashiyama, Director, Bob Jones Memorial Bible College (Quezon City, Philippines)

"Discerning God's will is the often puzzling—but necessary—task all Christians face. In *Planning Your Life God's Way*, Tim Berrey combines sound exegesis, biblical principles, and practical advice to help God's people from any walk of life in discerning and doing the will of God. If you are not sure of God's will for your life, reading *Planning Your Life God's Way* may be God's will for you."
Jared Garcia, Academic Director, Pines City Bible Baptist College (Baguio, Philippines)

"*Planning Your Life God's Way* challenged us that we should make God's will for our life as our goal because we are created in Christ Jesus unto every good work …. God is sovereign but we are responsible to seek and do of His good pleasure. In doing God's perfect, acceptable will, we find true blessedness and contentment."
Tang Tuck Keong, Senior Pastor, Jesus Saves Mission International (Singapore)

DEDICATION

To my Christian brethren in Singapore,
gracious first listeners
December, 2014

TABLE OF CONTENTS

ACKNOWLEDGEMENTS

My parents, Lloyd and Anita Berrey, lived as if obeying God's Word and doing His will were all that mattered in life. My seminary-days pastor, Mark Minnick, set me on what I still believe to be a biblical trajectory as it relates to decision-making and the will of God. My wife, Laura, and I have now for over fifteen years attempted to live (albeit imperfectly) what you find in this book and pass down its philosophy of life to our six children.

The good brethren of Jesus Saves Mission (Singapore) were the first to provide a venue to field-test this material as a series. Other opportunities to deliver the lectures (either in part or in whole) and further tweak the material followed at Bob Jones Memorial Bible College (Quezon City), Lighthouse Bible Believers Church (Parañaque), Pines City Baptist Church (Baguio), Chinese Fundamental Baptist Institute (Hong Kong), Faith Baptist Church (Queens, NY), and Calvary Baptist Church (Hampton, GA). It developed from there—my wife deserves the lion-share of the credit, humanly—into the product you now hold in your hand.

Susan Pritt, my mother-in-law, and Sarah Jackson, product editor, both worked hard to remove my errors in grammar and presentation. Frank Jones kindly agreed to serve as a theological sounding board, for which I am sincerely grateful. Paul Silas Julian, my student assistant, performed the thankless and tedious task of checking the accuracy of my verse references.

That this book still has defects is unfortunately a certainty (and no fault of theirs). I agree with Sir William M. Ramsay, the late New Testament scholar, who complained in one of his books (*The Bearing of Recent Discovery on the Trustworthiness of the New Testament*) that its deficiencies would rise up before him when it was too late.

On a different note, I have cited many different authors or persons in this book. Please do not consider my citation of them a full endorsement of all their beliefs or ministries. Every author or person that I have cited—and, in fact, everything that I myself have written in this book—must be held to the biblical maxim: *Test all things; hold fast what is good* (1 Thess. 5:21).

PREFACE

God is your Creator. You are not just a freak accident of evolution. You exist not simply because your mother wanted a baby. Or because your father wanted to try again for a boy. God desired your existence. That is why you came into this world, and that is why you continue in it. *You are worthy, O Lord, to receive glory and honor and power; for You created all things, and by Your will they exist and were created* (Rev. 4:11).

If God desires you to exist, then it follows naturally that your existence has a purpose. If God is sovereign, wise, all-powerful, and good, as the Bible depicts Him, then He does nothing randomly, illogically, or by accident.

For you particularly, who have been transformed by His grace through regeneration, it can be said that *everything works together for good* (Rom. 8:28). You have been *created in Christ Jesus for good works, which God prepared beforehand* for you to walk in them (Eph. 2:10). A certain sense of destiny haunts you. Something in you testifies that God has *fearfully and wonderfully made you* (Psa. 139:14). This is why you sometimes plunge into despondency: your current life does not match up with what you know you were created to be.

You stand at a crossroads. You can take your one life and let discouragement, sin, distraction, relationships, or any number of other things flush it into the realm of the insignificant. Or you can get to work planning your life God's way.

INTRODUCTION—
A LIFE WELL PLANNED

So teach us to number our days, that we may gain a heart of wisdom (Psalm 90:12)

Robert Dick Wilson (1856-1930) was twenty-five years old when he decided his life's work would be to defend the accuracy of the Old Testament. In accordance with that decision, he laid out his life's plan. Estimating that he would attain the age of seventy, and thus had another forty-five years ahead of him, he divided those forty-five years into three fifteen-year segments.

The **first fifteen years** he would learn every language in any way connected to the study of the Old Testament—languages such as Hebrew, biblical Aramaic, Greek, Latin, Syriac, Babylonian, Persian, Arabic, and Coptic. Language learning came easy to him. When a typhoid-like illness at age thirteen delayed his studies for two years, he "amused himself" (his words) by learning French. He spent one school vacation teaching himself German (scoring a one hundred percent when later tested on the subject); another, learning Spanish. He taught himself Italian, and then taught second-year Italian as an instructor. He collected languages the way some people collect stamps, and by the time he was done he was fluent in dozens of languages.[1]

The **next fifteen years** he would study the text of the Old Testament. He analyzed every consonant (over one million of them) in the Hebrew Old Testament, cross-examining them with the ancient Old Testament translations, such as the Septuagint, the Latin Vulgate, and the Syriac Peshitta.

He then determined that he would spend his **last fifteen years** sifting through the higher critical attacks on the Old Testament, rebutting them, and documenting the results of his years of research.

This was the life plan he laid out, and he stuck to it. Making the book of Daniel a focus because of critical notions against its historicity, Wilson published *Studies in the Book of Daniel* in 1916. He followed that in 1922 with *Is the Higher Criticism Scholarly?*, in which he rains down withering blows upon the assertions of those who attack the veracity of the Old Testament.

What is so helpful about Wilson's example?

First of all, he set himself a goal to which he would devote his life: to become a veritable one-man Department of Defense on behalf of the Old Testament. That goal was strategic. He took into consideration his unusual ability with languages and focused it on what he believed he could contribute to the kingdom of God. He could have harnessed his enviable language skills, put them out to work in the field of international diplomacy or business, and made a name for himself. Instead, he laid them on the altar of kingdom service.

Second, Wilson realized that in order to reach his goal, he had to have a concrete, measurable, relevant, and achievable plan. He saw that without a plan he would never reach his goal. He had only one life, and that one life must be budgeted. His goal—his life's priority— determined his forty-five-year life budget. His plan was concrete— learning Old Testament languages, for example. It was measurable—

every language in any way related to the Old Testament. It was relevant—how else can one defend the Old Testament if you are not an expert in all of its varied literature? And for him, even if not for us, it was achievable.

Third, Wilson streamlined his life. His father had wanted him to preach. Wilson himself enjoyed evangelistic work and had actually done so with some success; but he realized he could not both pastor and master the Old Testament in the way he desired. He did not allow himself to get sidetracked. *This one thing I do* did not hang in calligraphy on his office wall. It was branded with a hot iron onto his will and lived out with perseverance, diligence, zeal, and consecration.

Fourth, Wilson labored to see his plan brought to fruition and his goal realized. In the end, he could read any language even remotely associated with the Old Testament. He could reference any primary source a critical scholar might quote. He had scrutinized every consonant of the Old Testament. He could answer with authority any attack on the Old Testament.

Remember his goal of finishing his life's work by seventy years of age? Wilson authored a number of works, but arguably his greatest masterpiece, *The Scientific Investigation of the Old Testament,* was published in 1926, the very year he turned seventy. He accomplished his life's plan with remarkable precision.

Robert Dick Wilson exemplifies planning one's life God's way. Neither my life nor your life will look exactly like Robert Dick Wilson's; but when I look at his life, the word that comes to my mind is *blessed,* in the Old Testament sense of "Oh, to be envied."[2]

I envy a man who took such a realistic look at life. He openly acknowledged what so many people choose to blindly deny: that we have only a few useful years before our life will end in death. *So teach us to number our days, that we may gain a heart of wisdom* (Psa. 90:12). He also realized that although one person cannot do everything, he can accomplish *something* if he will focus his energy on that one thing.

I envy a man who took such a clear look at himself and who he was. He realized that his life's unique contribution to the kingdom of God would surely flow out of the unique gifting, background, and circumstances that comprised being Robert Dick Wilson. *I will praise You, for I am fearfully and wonderfully made; marvelous are Your works, and that my soul knows very well* (Psa. 139:14).

I envy a man who laid his remarkable gifting at the feet of Jesus his Savior and asked, *What shall I do, Lord?* (Acts 22:10).

I envy a man who disciplined himself to sweat through his life's plan and who actually achieved the goal he set for himself, crossing the finish line that he had designated forty-five years earlier. *I have fought the good fight, I have finished the race, I have kept the faith* (2 Tim. 4:7).

Don't you envy a man like that? Wouldn't you like to look back with satisfaction on a life well planned?

Here is the good news: your life can be just as enviable and fragrant with purpose as Robert Dick Wilson's. After all, the same God that ordered his steps will also order yours, if you will allow Him! *The steps of a good man are ordered by the LORD: and He delights in his way* (Psa. 37:23).

... You must, however, begin where Wilson began—by correctly answering life's "first question."

‹ 1 ›

ANSWER LIFE'S FIRST QUESTION

Follow Me, and I will make you become fishers of men (Mark 1:17)

In 1995, a Tampa surgeon made the news because he accidentally amputated the wrong leg of a patient. Everything told him he was cutting off the correct leg: the operating room blackboard, the operating room schedule, the hospital computer system, even the leg that had been sterilized and readied for the surgery. In the middle of the operation, too late to reverse the damage, the sobs of a nurse reviewing the patient's file alerted him to the fact that he was working on the wrong leg.[3]

Can you imagine making a mistake about something so serious? And yet, many people do. They actually make a mistake about their own life! They get their central mission in life wrong. Everything around them tells them they are doing the right thing: their friends, their colleagues, their relatives, their culture, even their instincts. But somehow, in the middle of a life lived for the wrong mission, they realize (almost too late) that they are pursuing the wrong thing. We all need to pause and ask ourselves, "Am I getting my mission right?"

What is your mission in life? The resolution to that query demands correctly answering a question that is logically prior. In fact, it is a question that I believe is one of life's most fundamental questions.[4]

WHO IS JESUS?

One day when my daughter was very young, we were riding home together. From her seat in the back of the car, her childish voice suddenly piped up and asked, "Daddy, what is Jesus?" As a two- or three-year-old, she had just stumbled upon life's chief question: "Who is Jesus?"

A good place to begin in answering that question is to read the Gospel of Mark. Mark takes his readers on a fast-paced journey through the earthly life and ministry of Jesus Christ. But it is his opening line that both startles and rivets the reader:

The beginning of the gospel of Jesus Christ, the Son of God (Mark 1:1).

In one short statement, Mark answers the most fundamental question, the question upon which hangs all of life's questions. Every man or woman must embrace the inescapable fact of who Jesus is—or face the harsh consequences.

When we affirm Jesus to be the Son of God, we are in no way implying some kind of conjugal relationship of the Father that resulted in a son. (This is a very common Muslim misunderstanding.) Instead, we are commenting on Jesus' nature and His relationship to the Father.

To affirm Jesus as the Son of God is to make a statement about His uniqueness. John 3:16, perhaps the best-known verse in the Bible, says as much when it refers to Jesus as the "only begotten Son."

For God so loved the world that He gave His only begotten Son, that whoever believes in Him should not perish but have everlasting life (John 3:16).

Unfortunately, the word "begotten" may conjure up in our minds a physical birth. Nothing could be further from the truth. "Begotten" (*monogenes*) literally means one of a kind or unique—"the only one of its kind or class."[5]

Believers in Jesus understand that they also are children of God—and rightly so—but in a far different sense than Jesus is. In fact, the expression "the Son of God," when the Greek word "son" is in the singular, occurs thirty-eight times in the New Testament and *always* refers to Jesus.[6] We could say it this way: God has many children, but He has only one Son!

Thus, to refer to Jesus as the Son of God is to affirm that He possesses the same divine nature as His Father. We get caught sometimes in squabbles with those from other religious persuasions, and we perhaps wish that the New Testament would state more clearly His full deity. Actually, it does! And in more ways than it is our purpose here to articulate.[7] But to call Him **the** Son of God is one of those ways. Just as my son is no less human than I am, so Jesus is no less God than His Father.

Mark does not leave you without proof of his assertion. His whole book essentially backs up his declaration, but his opening preface cannonades it at heart-stopping velocity.

Jesus, Mark's preface affirms, had a forerunner named John the Baptist (Mark 1:2-8). John's presence reiterates Jesus' uniqueness. Hundreds of years before Jesus' birth, the Old Testament predicted a Voice who would prepare the way for the Messiah through his preaching and teaching (Isa. 40:3).[8] We cannot exaggerate the importance of John's role as this Voice. Not that Jesus relied primarily on John's human witness to His veracity; He did not (John 5:34). Nonetheless, John's witness played a role in many believing on Jesus and is part of what distinguishes Jesus from so many religious imposters who have committed the fatal error of announcing themselves. They made great claims for themselves—an angel met them in a forest, or they saw a vision in a cave—but no one else was with them when these phenomena occurred. No independent verification exists. No forerunner announced their coming hundreds of years before it happened, and the Father definitely did not bear witness to their claims. In fact, in a few cases, these leaders relied on their followers to convince them of their alleged prophetic status. Not so with Jesus!

Mark's preface goes on to relate that an audible voice from heaven acknowledged and authenticated Jesus at the time of His baptism (1:9-11). John baptized multitudes of people, and the Galilean who came forward for baptism that day may have seemed like one of many. But John knew such was not the case. Other bystanders present on the occasion likely came away that day with the same conclusion. As Jesus came up out of the water, having submitted to the baptism of John, the Father audibly identified Jesus as *My beloved Son, in whom I am well pleased* (v. 11). In addition, the Holy Spirit descended upon Jesus—again in front of all onlookers—in the form of a dove. (One is struck by the pains taken to ensure that this occasion was audible and visible to all present.)

The Father's words imply an intimate ("beloved") relationship that clearly predates what took place in the Jordan River that day. They take us into eternity past before the Word took on human flesh in the man, Christ Jesus (John 1:1, 14). They remind us that the Son came to earth from heaven, where He had enjoyed the unending companionship of His Father.

No one has ascended to heaven but He who **came down from heaven**, *that is, the Son of Man who is in heaven* (John 3:13).

Well-known Christian apologist Ravi Zacharias assumes, for the sake of argument, that Mohammad really did visit heaven on one occasion.[9] He then counters by considering the claims of Jesus. Jesus did not boast that He was permitted, on merely one occasion, to visit heaven. Rather, Jesus claimed that He came from Heaven. And the Father's audible voice—to which all present that day could bear witness—authenticates Jesus' claim.

Mark, however, is still not done with his cannonade. He takes us still deeper into the identity of Jesus' person and the purpose of His coming when he speaks of Jesus' being driven into the wilderness and then tempted by Satan (vv. 12-13). Mark does not elaborate on Jesus' temptation, as the Gospels of Matthew and Luke do, but he tells us enough to suggest the stark loneliness of the event (the wild beasts were His only companions) and to imply His victory over Satan (why else would God have sent angels to minister to Him?).

This head-on, forty-day collision with Satan is another striking evidence to the unparalleled uniqueness of Jesus. Our Savior withstood all of Satan's broadsides, something no other person, from Adam to the present, had ever done. In fact, Jesus is the "last Adam" (1 Cor. 15:45), who came to rescue us from the plight into which we fell because of the first Adam.

To put it more bluntly, Jesus is the promised "Seed of the woman" who alone can crush the head of the serpent and deliver us from his clutches (Gen. 3:15). He is exactly what John the Baptist said He is: *The Lamb of God who takes away the sins of the world* (John 1:29). Jesus' uniqueness as the Son of God includes His winning for us a spectacular and much-needed battle over the sin that is literally killing each one of us. No religious deceiver has ever been able to do that or to come anywhere near to matching Jesus' words: *I don't have much more time to talk to you, because the ruler of this world approaches.* **He has no power over me** (John 14:30, NLT).

The great Egyptian pharaoh, Thutmose III (1479-1425 BC), once made the astonishing statement, "The god of heaven is my father. I am his son. He has begotten me, and commanded me to sit on his throne." His words sound almost like some that Jesus said. How could someone assess whether his claims were valid? Try this: his mummy is still with us. Thutmose claimed to be the son of God but he could not conquer death, the sting of sin (1 Cor. 15:56). He died, like every commoner in Egypt.

Jesus, on the other hand, conquered Satan, bore our sins as the Lamb of God, and then proved by His resurrection from the dead the validity of His claim to be the Son of God (Rom. 1:4).

Concerning His Son Jesus Christ our Lord, who was born of the seed of David according to the flesh, and declared to be the Son of God with power according to the Spirit of holiness, by the resurrection from the dead (Rom. 1:3-4).

JESUS AND YOUR LIFE'S MISSION

Now, what does this discussion about Jesus as the unique Son of God have to do with planning your life God's way or getting your mission right in life?

Everything!

The truth that Jesus is the unique Son of God carries with it a startling implication: there is no other great teacher or religious figure to whom we must listen or before whom we must bow. Affirming Jesus as THE Son of God narrows down all our religious options to one.

Nor is there salvation in any other, for there is no other name under heaven given among men by which we must be saved (Acts 4:12).

Jesus' unique status as God's Son demands a response. Only one response is logical, and it is the one that Jesus Himself urged upon those who would listen to Him:

The time is fulfilled, and the kingdom of God is at hand. **Repent, and believe** *in the gospel* (Mark 1:15).

Well-known author and former atheist Lee Strobel came to see this after a lengthy investigation into the claims of Jesus. He initially undertook the investigation in order to debunk his wife's newfound Christian faith. But when he locked himself in his office on November 8, 1981, after twenty-one months of research, the evidence in Christ's favor overwhelmed him. It would actually take more faith to remain an atheist, he realized, than to believe in Jesus.

The only sensible response was to bow the knee to the claims of Jesus and embrace Him as Lord and Savior. John's Gospel summarizes it this way:

But as many as received Him, to them He gave the right to become children of God, to those who believe in His name: who were born, not of blood, nor of the will of the flesh, nor of the will of man, but of God (John 1:12-13).

The crucial first step in getting right one's mission in life is becoming, through saving faith in Jesus, a child of God. The privileged status of becoming a child of God is not something you deserve nor something you earn as a product of your religious fervor. It is something that Jesus gives instantaneously to those who welcome Him in all of His glory as the unique Son of God, and believe in Him and the redemptive work He came to accomplish. The kind of faith we are describing is, to be blunt, both a human response and a divine miracle, as the juxtaposition of John 1:12-13 demonstrates. Verse 12 is the response demanded in order for you to become a child of God. Verse 13 reminds us that accompanying your response was the miracle of regeneration, as God birthed you into His family.

That miraculous—yet volitional—response of faith then launches you on a journey of discipleship in which you follow Jesus. To those early disciples who believed on Him, Jesus issued the following command: *Follow Me* … (1:17). His command still rings true for all His genuine disciples.

In fact, to speak of a disciple *following* is essentially redundant. Inherent in the word disciple is the idea of someone who is both a pupil and a follower. That is, he (or she) submits to the teaching of another, as their pupil, and then adheres to that teaching by following it himself. To not follow Him forfeits *de facto* the label disciple (Luke 14:27). In fact, any other response is absurd and unworthy of Him.

And he who does not take his cross and follow after Me is not worthy of Me (Matt. 10:38).

Those who follow Him then find themselves being transformed by Him. Jesus transforms them in a number of ways, but Mark's Gospel hones in on the one that will refocus their life's mission: *I will make you fishers of men* (1:17).

Jesus was setting before them the task that would dominate the rest of their lives. They were to follow Him, as His true disciples, and make disciples to Him of all others around them. No longer was their life to be wrapped up in fishing; they may have occasionally fished again vocationally, but it was no longer their life pursuit.

This radical mission—of being a disciple of Jesus and making disciples to Jesus—was not just for Jesus' first disciples. The Great Commission makes clear that it is obligatory for all Jesus' disciples.

And Jesus came and spoke to them, saying, "All authority has been given to Me in heaven and on earth. Go therefore and make disciples of all the nations, baptizing them in the name of the Father and of the Son and of the Holy Spirit, teaching them to observe all things that I have commanded you; and lo, I am with you always, even to the end of the age" (Matt. 28:18-20).

Every believer, as a follower of Jesus, is to make disciples of all those around him or her. They are to do so in every nation, in every age, in the power of the Spirit sent from heaven, with the conscious presence of Jesus aiding and urging them onward. If they get distracted from this by work, by a relationship, by wealth, or by anything else, they fail to get their mission right.

Getting distracted is easy to do, especially in an increasingly secular and materialistic world. I am convinced that we do not even realize how materialistic we are or how focused we are on this life's treasures, pleasures, and ideals. Too many of Jesus' disciples are content with carrying His name with them to the grave and living what many consider to be a "normal Christian life": church attendance (unless it conflicts with another priority), moderate obedience to God's Word, and pursuit of everything else that culture offers that is not flagrantly unbiblical.

This, however, is far from the "normal Christian life" lived out in the book of Acts. The early church had a very noisy faith. When it came to proclaiming forgiveness in the name of Jesus and calling all men to be His disciples, they could not be shut up. They had to declare it, and even when persecution landed them in far-flung places, they merely continued to shout their faith in a different location (Acts 8:4).

Getting your mission right will alter your view of everything: your talents, your time, your money, your relationships, your college education, your career, your marriage, your children, and your free time. Viewed correctly, all of these are simply Christ's gifts, stewarded by you, to bring Him the glory He deserves as you live and proclaim Him.

Think of it this way: you can die penniless or wife-less or childless or education-less, but you cannot leave this world disciple-less. You must follow Jesus, and you must be a fisher of men—or you have failed in getting your mission in life right. You have lived short of what Jesus' uniqueness as the Son of God deserves. You have robbed Him of the worship that He is due.

As you assess your life's objectives or ambitions, as you make daily decisions, as you anticipate what lies down the road for you, you absolutely must prioritize the mission of *following Jesus and bringing men and women to become followers of Him.* It should be one of the primary grids by which you assess the purchases you make, the hobbies you acquire, the places you live, the entertainment you choose, the relationships you build, and the jobs you hold.

Does that mean everyone should be in full-time vocational Christian service? Absolutely not! In fact, nowhere does the New Testament even hint at that. Most of the early church leaders probably worked a regular job. Perhaps one of the modern church's greatest failures has been the propagation of the idea that truly committed Christians go into full-time Christian service and the rest just work secular jobs. Fatal in that mindset is the implicit suggestion that those in full-time

Christian service are the ones who make disciples, as if those in secular careers are somehow not obligated to do so. That is not what Jesus intended at all! What He intended was that all of His disciples be involved in disciple making.

Does that mean everyone's life will look exactly the same? Of course not! Take two Williams, for example. Both believers. Both wanting their lives to count for Christ. Both Englishmen. Both born in the month of August. Both living and dying within a year or two of the other. However, Jesus' call to William Carey (1761-1834), the "father of modern missions," to follow Him looked a lot different than His call to William Wilberforce (1759-1833), the tireless abolitionist. Both, however, exhibited the transformation that following Jesus brings.

TIME FOR SELF-EVALUATION

Let me close this chapter with a seven-point checklist to use as a way of assessing whether you have successfully answered "Life's First Question." I composed this list to summarize the teaching of Mark's Gospel (all unspecified references are to his book) and to impress upon my own heart his clarion call for discipleship. Do you genuinely embrace all seven of these propositions? Are you living them?

(1) Everything about Jesus' life and ministry gives adequate witness to the truth of His claim to be uniquely the Son of God (1:1, 11; 3:11; 5:7; 9:7; 14:61; 15:39).

(2) Although He was the Son of God, He became man and compassionately poured Himself into serving wayward and needy mankind, helplessly ensnared as we are in the consequences of our evil actions (1:41; 2:17; 5:1-17; 6:34; 8:2).

(3) His ultimate act of service for mankind was to die on the cross as a ransom for them; that is, His shed blood paid the penalty demanded by God's offended justice because of our violations of God's laws (10:45; 14:24).

(4) God raised Jesus from the dead on the third day, clearly proclaiming that Jesus was the Son of God and that His death had fully satisfied God's offended justice (16:6; Rom. 1:4; 4:25).

(5) God offers eternal life to all those who will repent and believe this good news—that in Jesus God's kingdom has drawn near, and through Jesus all of God's promises of salvation are being fulfilled (1:15; 16:16). At the core of this good news ("gospel") is Jesus' death as a substitute payment for human sin, His burial, and His resurrection from the dead on the third day (8:31; 9:31; 10:33-34; 1 Cor. 15:3-4).

(6) Those who believe become Jesus' disciples, identifying themselves publicly with Him through water baptism and following Him (1:17; 16:16).

(7) In addition, Jesus' disciples live under the exciting obligation to preach this good news about Jesus to the entire world and call all mankind to become His disciples (16:15, 20).

… In answering life's first question, you have bowed the knee to Jesus as the Son of God; now get off your knees—or, better, stay there— and discover who He created you to be and why.

◀ 2 ▶

Read Your CV

I will praise You, for I am fearfully and wonderfully made (Psa. 139:14)

A t the Museum of Aviation in Warner Robins, Georgia, a whole room is dedicated to the memory of Robert L. Scott, Jr., one of the greatest American fighter pilots of World War II. Among a host of other accomplishments, Scott shot down at least thirteen Japanese planes. His flying skill was no accident. As a boy he longed to fly, and once tested a homemade glider off the copper roof of his neighbor's three-story house. His painful landing a few seconds later in some thorny rose bushes sixty feet below failed to dim in any way his passion to fly. For him, to live was to fly. His later exploits proved his intuition to be correct. How did he know that? It was written in his DNA, what I call a person's CV.

CV is an abbreviation for *Curriculum Vitae,* a Latin term that means "course of life." The Concise Oxford English Dictionary defines *curriculum vitae* as "a brief account of a person's education, qualifications, and previous occupations, typically sent with a job application." Americans generally refer to it as a "resume."

I am using the term "CV" metaphorically, to refer to a person's God-given uniqueness. We are not just some bubble of bacteria drifting aimlessly through an unsupervised cosmos. We have been specially crafted in the image of God, with particular gifts, personalities, opportunities, and circumstances.

In a world of over seven billion people, there is literally no one else like you. Your distinctive fingerprints only tell part of the story. In reality, all of you was constructed based on a unique blueprint.

BOW BEFORE YOUR DESIGNER IN WORSHIP AND SUBMISSION

Who you are reflects a Designer. In fact, it does not just reflect a Designer; it beams it, with a signal stronger than the world's most powerful radio emitter. This sense of purpose and calling is doubly clear for those who have been regenerated by the Spirit of God.

As a believer, you have a God who purposed from eternity past to call you to Himself through the gospel, to make you holy and like his Son, and to give you an inheritance. He has good works that He planned out in eternity past for you to do.

For we are His workmanship, created in Christ Jesus for good works, which God prepared beforehand that we should walk in them (Eph. 2:10).

While you were in the womb, He crafted you in a special way and fashioned your heart individually.

Before I formed you in the womb I knew you; before you were born I sanctified you; I ordained you a prophet to the nations (Jer. 1:5).

*He fashions their hearts **individually**; He considers all their works* (Psa. 33:15).

Your Designer crafted you strategically to accomplish a purpose and to glorify Him in a way that no one else can. A couple of authors have put it this way:

You were born prepacked. God looked at your entire life, determined your assignment, and gave you the tools to do the job. Before traveling, you do something similar. You consider the demands of the journey and pack accordingly. Cold weather? Bring a jacket. Business meeting? Carry the laptop. Time with grandchildren? Better take some sneakers and pain medication. God did the same with you….. God packed you on purpose for a purpose. Is this news to you? If so, you may be living out of the wrong bag.[10]

But who are we? And what is our destiny? Calling insists that the answer lies in God's knowledge of what he has created us to be and where he is calling us to go. Our gifts and destiny do not lie expressly in our parents' wishes, our boss's plans, our peer group's pressures, our generation's prospects, or our society's demands. Rather, we each need to know our own unique design, which is God's design for us.[11]

These authors are simply recognizing the truth of what David penned in Psalm 139.

For you formed my inward parts; you knitted me together in my mother's womb. I praise you, for I am fearfully and wonderfully made. Wonderful are your works; my soul knows it very well. My frame was not hidden from you, when I was being made in secret, intricately woven in the depths of the earth (vv. 13-15; ESV).

The Hebrew word translated "inward parts" (v. 13) literally means *kidneys*. When used metaphorically, it refers to the innermost part of man—more "inner" than even the heart of man. In other words, the deepest recesses of who you are were created by God.

David employs the imagery of knitting (v. 13) and weaving (v. 15) to describe how God formed your embryo into what you are today. Think of the care that goes into weaving a pattern on a blanket, the precision required to see the design worked through to its conclusion. With this same purposeful precision, God wove you when you were in your mother's womb. Do you remember every phone number you have

31

ever had? That's part of how God wove you. Maybe you cannot remember your current phone number, but you can picture a beautiful scene and capture it on canvas? Once again, that's God's knitting at work.

Our response to God's designer work should be a curious combination of praise—worshipful recognition of all God did when He formed us and the frank acknowledgement that He did a great job (v. 14)—and confidence—not a preening self-confidence, but the kind fostered by fathoming how strategically God designed you. No other human on earth can pull off as successfully the task you have been built to accomplish; you are, in this sense, irreplaceable.

But why? Why has God invested so much in your creation? Furthermore, why does He invite you to reflect on His creative genius? Psalm 139 would suggest that a **first** purpose is to bring Him praise. Have you ever praised God for the wonderful way in which He made you? Does this sound strange or smack of pride? Actually, it is worship: a candid confession of intelligent design; of a loving, sovereign Creator; and an incredible Architect.

Your eyes saw my substance, being yet unformed. And in Your book they all were written, the days fashioned for me, when as yet there were none of them. How precious also are Your thoughts to me, O God! How great is the sum of them (vv. 16-17)!

Second, reflecting on His creative genius should have the impact of making us take His side in a world of men who have chosen to reject Him.

Do I not hate them, O LORD, who hate You? And do I not loathe those who rise up against You? I hate them with perfect hatred; I count them my enemies (vv. 21-22).

Evolution is more than just a competing theory of life's origins in the marketplace of ideas. It is Satanically-deluded science fiction in which mankind emerges free from the shackles of accountability to a

Supreme Creator and proclaims himself master of his own fate. Sadly, the freedom acquired is a hollow victory. A sense of futility or pointlessness overshadows all attainments and leads only to despair.

Third, reflecting on God's creative genius should cause us to turn to Him in humble prayer and beg Him to point out every way in which we have used this body, His handiwork, to rebel against Him.

Search me, O God, and know my heart; try me, and know my anxieties; and see if there is any wicked way in me, and lead me in the way everlasting (vv. 23-24).

We should join the Psalmist in pleading for God to lead us into His way, the only way that leads to life eternal.

EMPLOY YOUR UNIQUENESS FOR HIS KINGDOM AND GLORY

God designed us wonderfully in order to use us strategically. Your uniqueness is what He will harness for His kingdom and glory. Amazingly, the moment we lay aside our arms of rebellion and allow Him to *lead us in the way everlasting* is the moment that we really start to live. Only then do we discover the answer to the question that almost every human being asks at some point in their life: "Why am I here on planet earth?"

When I first enrolled as a freshman at Bob Jones University, I signed up as an electronics engineering major. In retrospect, I find this amusing. I can fix hardly anything, and I am, quite frankly, afraid of electricity. When I surrendered my life to the Lord in January of 1989, He eventually led me to study for the ministry and has given me the privilege of teaching and preaching the Bible in numerous cultures and countries.

As I minister the Bible to differing audiences, I will sometimes complete a day of teaching and think to myself, "I was made to do this." I have found the reason God put me on planet earth.

Inspirational writer Max Lucado refers to this as the Christian's "sweet spot" and defines it as follows: "Using your uniqueness to make a big deal out of God every day of your life."[12]

Too many people have the idea that God's plan for their life will make them miserable.

One day, I was reading while several children were playing a game nearby. As I was reading, I occasionally picked up on various threads of their conversation. My ears really perked up when I heard a ten-year-old child say, with all dogmatic certainty, "Do you know what God's will is? Think of what you hate the most. That's God's will."

Unfortunately, his comment reflects the thinking of many. God's will is what you dread the most . . . on the level of eating asparagus or having a tooth pulled. To the contrary, God's plan for your life is found by discovering what you were made to do—those works that God prepared in advance for you and for which He designed you.

One of my former students in Bible college grew up with a real love for guns, knives, and all things military. When he felt God calling him to preach, he turned his back on an army career. It hurt; but after all, doesn't serving God cost you something? During his college years, a chapel speaker presented the need for chaplains in the military. As he listened, everything fell into place for him. God had called him to preach *and* intended him to use that calling in the military. He is currently serving as an army chaplain and has received high commendations because of his willingness to participate with his troops in all of their field maneuvers and munitions training.

His experience exemplifies the fact that God's will for your life is not necessarily predictable. That's part of the romance, the mystery, of being His. He may use you in a way that you could never have foreseen. What you will see, though—often in life's rearview mirror—is a creative Designer who is connecting the dots of your life uniquely and strategically. Virtually everything in your life is providential preparation for what lies ahead.

Squanto, the American Indian whom God used to save the lives of the courageous but unprepared *Mayflower* pilgrims, was one of the most traveled Indians of his day. Captured twice by British explorers, he crossed the Atlantic six times.

Through these unsolicited (and no doubt unwanted) circumstances, Squanto learned English and practical farming skills that enabled him to save the Plymouth colony. Squanto had little idea what lay ahead during his days as a virtual slave of British entrepreneurism, but God did! Providence was preparing him for a task far beyond what he could have imagined.

Similarly, you do not know what lies ahead, but your Creator-Designer does, and He specifically stocked *your* boat for your voyage over the horizon. Put that uniqueness to work for His kingdom![13]

After all, He is the source of your gifts, skills, background, personality, family, peculiarities, and wealth, and He desires that all of that display *His* glory and advance *His* kingdom. *What do you have that you did not receive* (1 Cor. 4:7)?

When William Wilberforce, the British politician we referenced briefly in the previous chapter, surrendered to Christ as a young adult, he at first felt it his duty to leave politics and enter the ministry. Wisely, however, he stayed in politics. He used his position of influence as a member of the British parliament to fight for the abolition of the slave trade in the British Empire. Politics became the arena of his greatest usefulness—the "sweet spot" where his uniqueness and God's kingdom intersected.

Wilberforce, like a host of others, looked at who he was—his created uniqueness—and put it to work for God's glory. Similarly, find what is in **your** hand—your CV—and employ it for the kingdom of God!

Whatever **your** *hand finds to do, do it with your might; for there is no work or device or knowledge or wisdom in the grave where you are going* (Ecc. 9:10).

BE CONTENT WITH WHO GOD CREATED YOU TO BE

Permit me to make a rather obvious observation: you cannot be everything. Basic though it may be, we do not always live it. We sometimes feel the pressure to consent to and excel in every opportunity that comes our way. We cannot. As one business guru puts it, we have to "prioritize until it hurts."[14] Scripture says it a little differently:

For I say, through the grace given to me, to everyone who is among you, not to think of himself more highly than he ought to think, but to think soberly, as God has dealt to each one a measure of faith (Rom. 12:3).

This admonition comes right after the command to present our bodies a living sacrifice (v. 1). A living sacrifice does not turn you into a superhero, able to do anything. Evaluate yourself honestly! Assess yourself, your circumstances, your opportunities, and your life according to the faith that God has given you. Author Gerald Sittser provides some helpful advice along this line:

> As if our present busyness is not enough, we feel pressure to accept new responsibilities, for we fear that we will miss out on something important or let someone down if we decline. Yet rarely do we consider the implications of the choices we make. Each new responsibility puts us deeper into the hole of distraction, stress, and overcommitment. When I am asked, for example, to speak at a weekend retreat in another city or state, I force myself to consider the hidden costs. Not only does the time away demand something from me, but also the time I need to prepare, the energy I must find to speak well and get to know the people there, the housework I will have to do when I return home, and the loss of a weekend I would have otherwise had with my kids. Strangely, I often feel guilty when I decline an invitation. I wonder sometimes what drives me to take on so many responsibilities, what makes me prone to be so busy, what deludes me into thinking I can do it all and have

it all. **I am like a man who is on a mission to everywhere** [emphasis mine].[15]

William Wilberforce, similarly, could not both enter the ministry and convince the British Parliament of the evils of the slave trade. He had to choose. We could learn from his wisdom. Neither you nor I can be on "a mission to everywhere."

The Apostle Paul was effective as a missionary because he kept his focus. He could never have planted churches all over four Roman provinces if he had stopped to pastor one of them or sidetracked himself in some other ministry endeavor. His one passion was to preach Christ where He had not yet been named. Paul knew what his calling was and he magnified it (Rom. 11:13). He did not overextend himself.

We, however, will not boast beyond measure, but within the limits of the sphere which God appointed us—a sphere which especially includes you. For we are not overextending ourselves (as though our authority did not extend to you), for it was to you that we came with the gospel of Christ (2 Cor. 10:13-14).

My wife and I have started a practice of going on a planning retreat every January in order to talk through our goals for the coming year. It has become a very helpful way to strategize. One year we determined that God wanted us to prioritize opportunities to strengthen families. Later in the year, we received two invitations to be in two geographically different locations at the same time. Which should we accept? One was to speak at a special Bible college function. The other was to address a singles retreat on the subject of Love, Courtship, and Marriage. Our goals for that year made our decision easy—the latter fit more closely with our stated focus.

We have a saying in English, "If you aim for nothing, you are sure to hit it." We could add that if you aim to do everything, you will accomplish nothing! Give thought to your steps (Prov. 14:15; ESV), and make sure that an opportunity or invitation is not actually detracting from God's main calling for your life.

Sometimes we are too busy. We tend to blame God, but often *we* are the ones who did not say "no." Is God opening those doors—or is it your ambition, pride, greed, or restlessness? Take a step back. Reassess your schedule. Re-read your CV.

Choose priorities and make plans in line with how God has uniquely gifted and designed you. Since the Lord is ordering your steps, you should see a sovereign "connecting the dots" at work in your life. Radical redirection is rare (and perhaps the result of stubbornness). The captain of a ship halfway to New Zealand will not normally reroute his ship toward Norway. Similarly, the Captain ordering each of your steps is following the course He has mapped out for you. He will not (often) reverse your ship overnight.

We alluded to William Carey in the previous chapter. His move from being a cobbler in England to a Bible translator in India may seem radical and disconnected, until you look a little more closely at his CV. He had from childhood evidenced an ability to never veer from a pursuit in which he engaged himself. His reading of books on travel had placed the world in his heart. Uneducated by society's standards, he had nonetheless managed to teach himself several languages. His study of Scripture confirmed to him God's desire to reach the world with the gospel. His conviction in that regard led to his speaking up in a ministers' conference and writing down his thoughts on the matter. His path then providentially crossed with a man already doing mission work in India. He himself went to India where, during a ministry that spanned over forty years, he translated all or portions of the Bible into thirty-three Indian languages and dialects.[16] Carey's surrender to go to India and his eventual usefulness there were actually the culmination of years of connecting the dots. Yes, in a direction no doubt unanticipated in his younger years, but in a way that nonetheless fit with how God was steering his ship.

On the other hand, if it is *we* who are trying to change course, we may find our Pilot realigning the helm back to its previous setting. A friend of mine in the banking industry really wanted to teach the Bible on the mission field. He made a trip to Asia, contemplated another, started taking theological classes, found he did not have the time, and stuck with his job in finance! His ambition to teach Bible overseas was noble, even sacrificial, but he eventually perceived that was not how God was connecting the dots of *his* life.

Resist the temptation of wanting to be like somebody else. We seem to have an innate discontentment with who God created us to be. God, however, did not pack us to live out of somebody else's bag. He packed you in the way that He did on purpose. Nobody else can live out of your suitcase the way you can. Choose to live out who God created *you* to be. Embrace *your* CV!

We come back again to the main theme of this chapter—you were created unique, and it is that uniqueness that God will use strategically for His glory. God did not design you to fly somebody else's plane or sail somebody else's boat. Just because it was "right" for someone else does not mean it is right for you.

Joseph's story was to remain in Egypt; Moses' was to refuse it. James' story was to be the first of the Twelve to die a martyr; his brother John's, to be the last. Ezra's story was to trust God for safety *without* an official escort; Nehemiah trusted God by having one. Ezra expressed his frustration with sinfulness by pulling out his own hair; Nehemiah, by yanking out the hair of others. Stephen preached and died; Paul escaped in a basket. God healed Epaphroditus, but refused to remove Paul's thorn in the flesh.

One Old Testament scholar has observed that Abel walked with God and died. Enoch walked with God and never died. Noah walked with God and everyone else died. "We cannot dictate where faith will lead."[17] Our individual stories are not "one size fits all" (and neither are most shirts that say they are).

In *The Horse and His Boy* by C. S. Lewis, Aslan takes a few moments during a lull in the action to explain to Shasta how everything in Shasta's life had been providentially overseen by himself. But when

Shasta asks him a question about Avaris' life, Aslan refuses to answer. *"Child,"* said the Lion, *"I am telling you your story, not hers. No one is told any story but their own."*

We each have a story, planned from start to finish by a loving, all-knowing, all-powerful God. Call it what you will—your God-designed uniqueness, your CV, or your "sweet spot"—all of this is code language for God's working in and preparing you to do the works which He planned out in advance for you.

‹ **3** ›

Maximize Your Life

Therefore do not be unwise, but understand what the will of the Lord is (Eph. 5:17)

The pilot swung the plane left and then banked right until we were headed due west. We continued our descent until the wheels touched the runway, and I was once again on the island of Mindanao. Nobody was waiting to pick me up. I had flown in to the airport a few times before—I had assured my pastor-friend—and would just take an airport shuttle bus directly to the mall in town, where he could pick me up. It would save him the hour-long trip to the airport.

Just outside the terminal were the stalls where the various shuttle personnel loudly clamored for the attention of exiting passengers, as if the higher the volume of their voice, the higher the quality of their shuttle. I shunned the noisier booths with the longer lines and walked up to a quieter booth. The fare was the same as the others, and I soon found myself sitting in one of its shuttles. It was a van—not a bus—and quite comfortable. I settled back to enjoy the quick trip to the mall.

Then we began making stops. First, at a hotel that I did not recognize. Then a residential area. Then a mall in the wrong part of the city.

Somewhat dismayed, I realized that I had unintentionally chosen the door-to-door shuttle instead of the direct one. It eventually made it to the mall where my friend was patiently ticking off the minutes, but definitely not at the time I had specified.

I resolved never again to use that same shuttle transport company. The first time, I could at least blame the fact that I did not know better. For me to choose the shuttle a second time would be a foolish waste of time.

DON'T BE FOOLISH!

It would be the same kind of foolishness that Paul has in mind when he admonishes those at Ephesus, *Therefore do not be foolish, but understand what the will of the Lord is* (5:17).

Paul's chief point in this section of Ephesians (vv. 15ff) is that a believer must walk very carefully, as someone who is wise (not unwise). The word *wise* (v. 15) describes someone who has received insight "into known facts." In the context of Ephesians, the insight given is insight into the "true nature of God's plan."[18] Because we (as believers) have been given insight into God's plan, we must walk very carefully. We do so by *making the most of our time* (v. 16; NASB). Those who walk carefully will not waste any opportunity that comes their way. The need to seize every opportunity is great *because the days are evil*. The days are evil chiefly because Satan is the *god of this age* (2 Cor. 4:4). Because of him, we live in a cursed world where life is fragile, our flesh is strong, and we war incessantly against principalities. Satan will do his best to make sure we never get a second opportunity if we pass the first one up.

All of this (in Eph. 5:15-16) leads up to the conclusion Paul arrives at in verse 17. At first glance, the word *foolish* reminds us of the words *wise* and *unwise* that we saw in verse 15. However, the Greek word used here is different from the word(s) used in verse 15 and actually builds upon them. The word *foolish* in verse 17 does not refer to someone who has no insight but to someone who is failing to use the insight they have. They have insight but are not applying it and, therefore, lack discernment. To allude back to the illustration with which I opened this chapter, it would be like my jumping on the same door-to-door airport shuttle that so delayed me the first time. Now that I have insight about the nature of that shuttle, I would be lacking in discernment (foolish) to use it again.

APPLY SCRIPTURE TO YOUR LIFE

Rather than be foolish, a believer is to *understand what the will of the Lord is.* To understand is to mentally grapple with something until it "challenges one's thinking or practice."[19] The *will of the Lord* is a synonym for the will of God, which occurs in Ephesians five times (1:1, 5, 9, 11; 6:6). Each time it describes something God wants. God wanted Paul to be an Apostle (1:1). He wanted to predestine us to adoption and to an inheritance (vv. 5, 11). He wants (and will bring) everything into submission to the Lordship of Jesus (v. 9). He wants slaves to obey their masters from the heart (6:5-6). The safest and surest source for a believer to find what God wants is God's Word, for it is there that God has revealed insight into His plan. To keep His commandments (in His Law) is to walk in His ways.

Therefore you shall keep the commandments of the LORD your God, to walk in His ways and to fear Him (Deut. 8:6).

Paraphrasing the whole verse (Eph. 5:17) yields something like this: do not foolishly fail to apply the insight into God's plan that you have; rather, make application of Scripture to your life circumstances until it (Scripture) challenges your thinking and practice.

We have one spectacularly messy closet in our house where we store our board games. We have games that range in length from fifteen minutes to several hours. Sometimes when we are preparing to run an errand or leave for church, I will announce to my children, "Be 100% ready to go. We are leaving in fifteen minutes." It never ceases to amaze me how, on the heels of that announcement, my children will pull out a two-hour game like Risk or Monopoly—games that can easily take a full fifteen minutes just to set up. I have given them insight into my plan for the family, but they are not fleshing out that insight in their actions. They lack discernment.

HOW TO NOT WASTE YOUR LIFE

Ephesians 5:15-17 unlocks a key (perhaps several of them) to planning your life God's way. Failing to make real-time application of an old-time book is foolishness. "True godliness is not the outward conformity to God's law but the spiritual application of God's law to one's life by God himself."[20] You will waste your time—and ultimately your life—if you do not discern how Scripture applies to you.

David understood that knowing God's ways demanded more than mere head knowledge. In Psalm 25, David prays that God would *cause him to know* God's ways and *teach him God's paths* (v. 4). Obviously, David is praying that God would help him to know God's ways *as they are found in His Word.* We sense, however, something deeper in David's prayer than just intellectual comprehension. He is crying out for the ability to apply to his own pathway what He discovers in Scripture about God and His ways: "teach me to know how your ways and my life intersect." *I thought about my ways, and turned my feet to Your testimonies* (Psa. 119:59).

Later in Psalm 119, David rejoices before the Lord because of the understanding the Word of the Lord has given him. His meditation on God's Word has made him wiser than his enemies (vv. 97-98). He has more understanding than his teachers and the aged (vv. 99-100), and he avoids turning from God's rules to evil and false ways (vv. 101-104).

The understanding he exults in is not mere head knowledge; rather, it is the God-given discernment to live his life God's way. He has experienced in real time that Scripture is *a lamp to his feet and a light to his path* (v. 105).

Nehemiah also allowed God's Word to *light his path*, when he led the post-exilic community of his day into a covenant to obey the Law of God (Neh. 9:38; 10:29). The Law had been given by Moses, but they applied it to themselves personally: **we** will not give our sons and daughters to the peoples of the land (10:30). They did not just obey "exact commands" (like the one above not to intermarry with the peoples of the land); they also applied the Law to their situation. For example, the Law forbids work on the Sabbath. They inferred that to mean no buying (which involved some work for them and more work for the seller) on the Sabbath, and they covenanted not to purchase from any neighboring peoples who sold merchandise or grain on the Sabbath (v. 31). The Law specifies that a fire must be kept burning at all times on the bronze altar. Nehemiah and company ensured compliance by setting up a system for sharing the responsibility to contribute wood to be burned (v. 34). They summarized the essence of their covenant burden in the closing words of the chapter: *we will not neglect the house of our God* (v. 39). No such exact command is found in the Law (the closest is perhaps the command not to neglect the Levite [Deut. 12:19; 14:27]), but that was their personalized application of the Pentateuch ordinances for Tabernacle worship.

My point is that they found God's will in His Law and meditated on it in order to make application to their day—until it challenged (and changed) their thinking and behavior. This kind of meditation is precisely what Joshua was admonished to do as he took on the colossal task of leading the children of Israel across the Jordan River and into the Promised Land. Joshua was not just to meditate on the Law's contents; he was to meditate on *how* to obey it.

This Book of the Law shall not depart from your mouth, but you shall meditate in it day and night, that you may **observe to do** *according to all that is written in it. For then you will make your way prosperous, and then you will have good success* (Josh. 1:8).

I hope you can see at this point how key Ephesians 5:15-17 is to the whole task of planning your life God's way. Follow again the logic of these three verses: You have been given insight into God's plan. Accordingly, you now have the ability (and duty) to walk carefully. Do so by making the most of your opportunities. The days are evil so to waste an opportunity is probably to lose it forever. Walking carefully in this way will require discernment on your part to apply God's will to your unique life circumstances. To do otherwise would be foolishness—an utter waste of your time and opportunities.

HOW TO WASTE YOUR LIFE

In summary, the surest way to waste your life is to fail to apply the Word of God to it. You will not know what opportunities are from God or how to seize those you do have.

I once read the story of a pastor's wife who thought she would surprise her husband by re-organizing his books for him. She picked a day when he was out and went to work: diligently matching books of the same color and same size, regardless of the books' contents. The husband came home to find the books on his shelves in a visually attractive arrangement but one completely unusable. The wife had unintentionally (and with good motives) wasted her own time and, ultimately, also her husband's because she had not clarified first what her husband *wanted* with regard to the arrangement of his books.

Similarly, when you fail to *understand what the will of the Lord is,* you will not walk carefully—like someone should who has been given the insight into God's plan that you have (as His child)—and you will not use to the maximum the life you have. Product of God's creative genius as you may be, you will waste your life on the altar of unapplied Scripture if you do not heed Paul's admonition here in Ephesians 5:15-17.

… Maximizing your life sounds exciting, but it requires a level of discernment that not everyone has.

‹ **4** ›

Transform Your Discernment

Prove what is that good and acceptable and perfect will of God (Rom. 12:2b)

She was a young mother of preschool-aged children. Tired of her current job, which seemed to her like drudgery, beset by financial woes, and frustrated with domestic problems, she decided to leave her family behind and apply for a job in another country.

My wife and I looked at her in dismay when she told us of her plan. It seemed, in every way, to lack discernment.

"Have you asked your pastor?"

"No, he will not approve," she answered.

"What does your husband think?"

She hesitated before she replied. "He says I can do whatever I want."

"Do you truly think this is God's will for your life?"

She shrugged. "It's what I want to do."

We counseled her not to leave her family, but her mind was made up. She didn't care what we said; she didn't care what her pastor thought. When we shared some Scripture with her about God's will for wives and mothers, she shrugged those verses off also.

What was her primary problem? Was it that God's Word lacked clear direction or was it a conflict of interests in her own heart?

Her example reminds us that there are certain prerequisites that are necessary in order to make real-time application of God's Word to our lives. If those prerequisites are not in place in our lives, then we are not able to discern correctly what God wants for us.

Planning our life God's way does not begin with a list of decisions to make, places we want to go, or goals we want to accomplish, but rather with a personal spiritual inventory: what kind of person are you? *whose* are you? who or what controls your thinking? Not even ensuring you have a Bible in your hand is enough.

The mother in the story above had a Bible! But there was something more fundamental missing—a discernment that would enable her to read and apply Scripture to her life. What would transform her (and our) discernment?

Paul gives the answer in a passage familiar to many Christians:

I beseech you therefore, brethren, by the mercies of God, that you present your bodies a living sacrifice, holy, acceptable to God, which is your reasonable service. And do not be conformed to this world, but be transformed by the renewing of your mind, that you may prove what is that good and acceptable and perfect will of God (Rom. 12:1-2).

We often focus on his opening exhortation to *present your bodies a living sacrifice* or on his imperative to *not be conformed to this world*. We forget that these commands are linked to a final purpose—*in order that you may prove those good, acceptable, and perfect things that are truly God's will* (my paraphrase).

In other words, a surrendered body and a transformed mind are what enable us to discern what things around us partake of the qualities *good, acceptable*, and *perfect* and, therefore, are the will of God. Without surrender and transformation, we are likely to mislabel the bad good and the unacceptable acceptable.

CHARACTERISTICS OF GOD'S WILL

After all, what is the determiner of what is good? Your desires? Your culture? What your parents did? What gets the most likes on Facebook? What your conscience tells you is okay?

(1) God's will is good

Not everything we view as good is truly good. One day my wife was working in the kitchen when she heard a scream from our two-year-old twins. She looked up from her baking to see that they were fighting over an open pair of scissors. One of the twins, while trying to yank them away from his brother, was actually closing the blades on the hand of his twin. My wife practically vaulted the kitchen table to get to them. The twin who gripped the handles gave the scissors up willingly. The other twin, still clutching the bare blades, tried to keep her from confiscating them. Even though blood flecked his palms, he clutched them tightly in his hands and screamed for his right to play with them. Why? Playing with naked blades seemed good to him. The nerve of his mother to rob him of such joy!

Similarly, the two-year-old son of friends of ours has developed a love relationship with electric fans. What neater toys have ever been invented? When they rescue him from the fan (or the fan from him), he yells and screams as if they are depriving him of his chief pleasure in life. He has no understanding yet of the devastating impact that a fan blade can have on a chubby baby finger.

Unfortunately, we do not always increase in wisdom as we age. Even as adults, we often think something is intrinsically good when it is not.

- ▹ We view a job as good because it pays well, without considering the effect it will have on our spiritual lives when we miss church regularly.

- ▹ We enjoy the companionship in a relationship without reflecting on the carnage to our character.

- ▹ We judge a university or a course of study by the job power we will draw as a graduate, not by the spiritual damage it will do to our souls.

- ▹ We savor a movie because of the way it makes us feel, and overlook the flawed worldview it is communicating to our conscience.

Here's the point: God's will is always that which is good. Genuinely good. One-hundred-percent good. The best! This truth can comfort us in times of unanswered prayer. God sometimes denies our requests because He knows that we are asking for a stone, although we may *think* we are asking for bread (Matt. 7:9). He knows it is not truly good for us, and therefore He does not grant it. We must avoid insisting on our own way so stubbornly that God responds as He did to Israel, when He gave them their request *but sent leanness to their soul* (Psa. 106:15).

(2) God's will is acceptable

Another characteristic of God's will is that it is "acceptable." This term is consistently used in the New Testament to refer to that which is well-pleasing in God's sight (Rom. 14:18; 2 Cor. 5:9; Eph. 5:10; Phil. 4:18; Col. 3:20; Heb. 13:21). Here also it reminds us that God's will consists of those things that please Him. The first question we must ask is not what pleases *me*, but what pleases *Him*. Nothing that displeases God can be His will.

The worn-out adage, "One man's trash is another man's treasure," acknowledges the reality that people do not view things from the same perspective. We grow up with strong food preferences, enjoying some flavors and viewing others as disgusting. We have decided opinions about which sports are the most entertaining or which politicians are most honest or what clothes suit us best.

Similarly, not everything that you like is what God likes. The Scripture provides us with clear examples of those things that God cherishes and those things that grieve Him. We did not compile the list; He did. No matter how much we might like it or think it might be okay with God, no matter how many of our friends agree with our sentiments, if it goes against God's stated likes and dislikes, it is not His will.

(3) God's will is perfect

Finally, Romans 12:2 declares that God's will is "perfect." One of the most quoted Greek lexicons in use today has this definition for "perfect": *attaining an end or purpose.*[21] We often use the word perfect in this way. For example, my wife will rummage after dinner through her Tupperware containers for something to store the leftovers in. When she finds one that is exactly the correct size, she will say, "That is perfect!"

The 2002 Hyundai van our family owns is far from blemish-free. A pastor once asked me if thoughtless people had ever put a dent in it. I wanted to tell him, "No, but my kids have." Scooters, bicycles, skateboards, countless balls, and who-knows-what-all have scratched it, hit it, and bounced off it. It bears multiple war wounds. But when my wife and I talk about the van, we say it is "perfect" for our family. Why? It accomplishes the purpose of transporting the eight of us and all of our varied belongings.

Just as our van accomplishes perfectly my purpose (in having a family vehicle), even so that which is God's will accomplishes His. The will of God is *perfect* in that it attains His exact end or purpose in your life. You cannot improve in any way on what God wants for you.[22] Obviously, then, we need to know something of His ends. This requires insight into His plan (per the previous chapter) and the discernment to make real-time application to our fast-paced twenty-first century lives.

PROVING WHAT IS GOD'S WILL

These three characteristics—good, acceptable, and perfect—are what our passage singles out as the content of "what God wants us to be and to do."[23] But how are we to know what in our lives and circumstances exhibits those three?

We are to *prove* them (v. 2). To prove has the idea of approving something after you have examined it. We are to examine who we are and what we do, and see if it matches up with what Scripture proclaims as good, acceptable, and perfect. Give your life a stringent test, using the Bible as the plumb line.

Making this kind of scrutiny, however, carries with it a certain underlying assumption: the *ability* to examine. Consider these two passages (both from Luke's Gospel) that use the same Greek word translated *prove* in Romans 12:2.

*Hypocrites! You can **discern** the face of the sky and of the earth, but how is it you do not **discern** this time?* (12:56).

*And another said, "I have bought five yoke of oxen, and I am going to **test** them. I ask you to have me excused"* (14:19).

Those who would discern the weather must have some prior acquaintance with climatic phenomena in their area. A buyer must have the necessary experience to examine *satisfactorily* his newly-acquired ox.

Personally, I would have no clue what to look for in an ox. I would assume that if he eats, snorts, smells, and kicks anybody who comes near, he will be belligerent enough to accomplish the job that I bought him to do. How much more qualified is someone who knows cattle and knows what to look for in a good ox!

Now (to turn back to our passage in Romans 12), what enables us to discern those objects or pursuits around us that are inherently good, genuinely well-pleasing to the Lord, and perfect?

PREREQUISITES FOR PROVING GOD'S WILL

I beseech you therefore, brethren, by the mercies of God, that you present your bodies a living sacrifice, holy, acceptable to God, which is your reasonable service (v. 1).

The discernment to make God-honoring decisions necessitates the surrender of your body to God as a living sacrifice. (This act of surrender assumes that you have experienced God's mercies in salvation, so eloquently set forth in Romans 1-11.) Before you can prove what is or what is not God's will, you must lay down your arms of rebellion. This is not just an act of mystical or abstract spirituality. God refers to our bodies as the "body of sin" (Rom. 6:6). If you think about it, our bodies are what give physical hands and feet to the temptations that Satan hurls our way! Jesus even made the shocking recommendation that it is better to have only one eye or one hand than to reap the eternal condemnation of a body which has given sway to sinful enticement (Matt. 5:29-30).

In order to make any progress in discerning the good, well-pleasing, and perfect in your real-time circumstances, you must submit your traitorous body to the Lord. If we succeed in discerning what God's will is, "it is in large measure because we have clarity about our ultimate allegiance."[24] How will we ever truly discern God's will if our ears still belong to the enemy? How will we ever truly discern how to use our eyes for the glory of God if we have never fully yielded their use to the God who gave them to us?

In addition, Romans 12 continues, you must maintain a decidedly non-conformist position toward the world:

And do not be conformed to this world, but be transformed by the renewing of your mind (v. 2a).

The Greek word itself for "world" (*kosmos*) suggests something of the world's organized or systematic nature. This organized system is not morally neutral but is actually in direct opposition to the Father.

*If anyone loves the world, the love of the Father is not in him. For all that is in the world—the lust of the flesh, the lust of the eyes, and the pride of life—is **not of the Father** but is of the world* (1 John 2:15-16).

The world draws us into its tentacle-like embrace by stimulating desires (*lusts*) that are in opposition to what God would want. These desires are essentially three-fold: Indulge! Acquire! Achieve!

God emphasizes self-control, prudence, and personal discipline; the world beckons us to indulge our desires (*lusts of the flesh*). God warns of covetousness and jealousy; the world summons us to listen to our eyes and hit the buy button (*lusts of the eyes*). God cautions against pride, selfishness, and smug self-dependence; the world assures us that we can accomplish our dreams and that, in fact, we deserve to succeed (*pride of life*).

All the bling the world flashes before our eyes is temporary (1 John 2:17), although it may not feel so at the moment of appeal. Everywhere we go, the world beckons us. Walk the mall and you will be bombarded by life-size posters of beautiful people who are all wearing the same expensive brand of watch. The message numbs our brains: if you indulge yourself—if you buy the same watch they did—you also will be stunning and successful. This is exactly the point of Romans 12:2: we must decide that we will not allow the world's glitter to shape our desires.

One of the billboards in the Philippines makes me chuckle every time I see it. On it, a movie actor, minus his shirt, is holding up a can of Century brand tuna. It's almost like he is saying, "Eat Century tuna and you can look like me. Take off your shirt and try it." Tuna just never struck me as macho-man food.

If you think about it, our world abounds with ridiculous slogans:

- ▷ It doesn't get any better than this. (Budweiser)

- ▷ Have it your way. (Burger King)

- ▷ I'm lovin' it. (McDonalds)

- ▷ Save Money. Live Better. (Walmart)

- ▷ The happiest place on earth. (Disneyland)

Slogans like these remake you into their image, the very conformity to the world that Romans 12:2 warns against. But here is the big problem with that conformity: it is one of the greatest hindrances to identifying what God wants.

Adulterers and adulteresses! Do you not know that friendship with the world is enmity with God? Whoever therefore wants to be a friend of the world makes himself an enemy of God (James 4:4).

Those conformed to the world's slogans cannot possibly prove what is good, well-pleasing to the Lord, and in line with God's perfect purposes. The world will sell you down the river for treasures, pleasures, and ambitions that come far short of God's standard of "perfect," but you will never know it because you have bought into its corrupt agenda. We absolutely must have (to return to our text in Romans) a transformed mind. *Be transformed by the renewing of your mind* (12:2b). When Paul speaks of "renewing of the mind," he is talking in moral or spiritual terms, not in terms of intelligence.

The Psalmist said it this way: *How can a young man cleanse his way? by taking heed according to Your word* (119:9). Christ said, *You are already clean because of the word which I have spoken to you* (John 15:3). Paul reminds us that Christ cleansed the church *with the washing of water by the word* (Eph. 5:26).

As the Spirit of God teaches you spiritual truths from the Word of God, your mind is renewed and you experience radical personal transformation. Without this transformation, a person simply cannot discern what the will of God is.

"No one discovers the line of action which from possessing these characteristics [good, acceptable, perfect] can be identified as the will of God unless he is transformed from his native affinity to the world by the renewing of his mind by the Holy Spirit."[25]

Constant absorption desensitizes. Chain cigarette smokers are around the smell of tobacco smoke so much they do not even notice it. But when they have quit and been away from its strong pungent odor, they will once again notice it when they enter a room filled with it.

Similarly, as long as we are living in conformity to the world's slogans, we will not detect anything wrong with their messages. Discernment follows transformation, enabling us to view more accurately what we formerly were immersed in and slaves to.

Remember your first pair of glasses? Trees, formerly longish blurry-green blobs, now sported individual branches and leaves. Flowers sprouted petals, street signs letters. The world looked entirely different. Similarly, regeneration and the ongoing cleansing of the Word give a person spiritual glasses through which he or she now views the world in a different light. *Old things have passed away; behold, all things have become new* (2 Cor. 5:17b).

A TRANSFORMED YOU

All of this points us back to where we started: you must be the right kind of person if you wish to discern what kinds of things are God's will. Have you genuinely surrendered your physical body to the Lord? Have you crucified its desires?

Therefore do not let sin reign in your mortal body, that you should obey it in its lusts (Rom. 6:12).

But put on the Lord Jesus Christ, and make no provision for the flesh, to fulfill its lusts (Rom. 13:14).

Who or what is shaping your desires? If worldly desires have enslaved your body, you will not be able to discern what God's will is.

Is your mind being renewed? Are you growing in your Scriptural knowledge and discernment so that you are loving things truly worth loving and choosing things that are genuinely worth choosing?

And this I pray, that your love may abound still more and more in knowledge and all discernment, that you may approve the things that are excellent, that you may be sincere and without offense till the day of Christ (Phil. 1:9-10).

… A good test of where our loyalties lie and whether our discernment has been transformed is to examine our response to that which God has explicitly revealed in His Word to be His will.

◄ 5 ►

Master the Fundamentals

I delight to do Your will, O my God (Psa. 40:8)

For much of the 2015-2016 NBA season, Stephen Curry wowed crowds with his unparalleled long-distance shooting. He even managed to drop in enough half-court-and-beyond bombers to convince us of his prowess. But soon court casters began to zoom in on his pre-game drills. Fans would show up early just to watch it. Why? Curry would spend some twenty minutes just dribbling the basketball, shooting from every imaginable angle, and anticipating the pressure he was likely to feel from the defense. Curry realized that the key to greatness on the court is a mastery of the fundamentals of the sport.

In some ways, this chapter is about reminding ourselves of the fundamentals. We often find ourselves charmed with the special, the spectacular, and the supernatural, to the point where we overlook the importance of the ordinary. This is like a basketball player who labors to win the slam dunk contest but neglects the fundamentals of dribbling, passing, and shooting. He will not go far in the NBA!

Likewise, to plan our lives God's way we must cultivate the fundamental of a heart that longs to obey what God has clearly revealed in His Word.

Oh, that they had such a heart in them that they would fear Me and always keep all My commandments, that it might be well with them and with their children forever (Deut. 5:29)!

God longs for such a heart of obedience in His children today!

Where does one begin in cultivating a heart of obedience? We must start by looking up verses that state explicitly what God wants. To create this chapter, I combed through the New Testament and studied all the references that related to God's wanting, wishing, or willing. My goal was to come up with a list of those things that God has revealed that He desires. I then sorted the references I found and categorized them into the ten statements below.

(1) God wills that His will always be done on earth.

In the second petition of the Lord's Prayer, Jesus teaches His disciples to pray for God's will to be *done on earth as it is in heaven* (Matt. 6:10). Prayer for what God wants to be done on earth is something one can always pray for with confidence. Why? Because God's will is that His will always be done! Basic as this aphorism may be, it is often disregarded in actual practice.

Sometimes, I will give my children specific instructions about what I want them to do. I will say something like, "Tonight is reading night. I want everyone in bed by 8:30 pm. Once in bed, you may read any book of your choice." Inevitably, one of them will ask, "Daddy? Can we play a game?" Or perhaps I will stipulate that the kind of function we are attending requires a collared shirt. In spite of my clear instructions, I will get the question, "Daddy? Can I wear a t-shirt?" How often do we do this to God? We read what God has clearly revealed in His Word about His will, and then we proceed to ask Him for an exception.

Christ came to do (and did) the Father's will (John 4:34; 5:30; 6:38). David was a man who did all God's will (Acts 13:22; cf. v. 36). Paul was chosen by God to know God's will (Acts 22:14). Christ's closest relatives are those who do God's will (Matt. 12:50; Mark 3:35).

Those who do God's will abide forever (1 John 2:17); in the end, it is only those who do the Father's will (and not just profess to) who will enter heaven (Matt. 7:21). This is the opposite of how we lived prior to our salvation: we obeyed the will of **our** flesh and mind (Eph. 2:3) and were captives of Satan to do **his** will (2 Tim. 2:26).

It is worth repeating: It is *always* God's will that we obey His will. And neither you nor I—regardless of the unique or unusual circumstances we face—are the grand exception to that. God's faithfulness ensures that He will never allow a situation to arise in which we are "ethically required" to disobey one of His rules.

No temptation has overtaken you except such as is common to man; but God is faithful, who will not allow you to be tempted beyond what you are able, but with the temptation will also make the way of escape, that you may be able to bear it (1 Cor. 10:13).

Too many people rationalize disobedience by quipping, "God will understand," as if God would take their side if He only had a chance to hear their defense. Job, at one point, felt this way. He was not excusing disobedience, but he was frustrated over what he perceived to be unfair treatment and he felt that things would turn out differently if he could just explain his case before God. However, when God finally came to him, Job reversed himself. He decided that *he* had uttered things he did not understand (Job 42:3).

If Job's case was not an exception to the rightness of God's ways, neither yours nor mine will be either. Best to repent like Job did and marvel at the mysterious ways of our good, omniscient, and omnipotent God! God—not you or I—will be justified on that great day *when God will judge the secrets of men by Jesus Christ* (Rom. 2:16).

(2) God wills your creation and your ongoing existence and, therefore, deserves all glory, honor, and power.

Revelation 4 is a powerful chapter that ushers us right into the heavenly throne room. The very last verse puts us and everything around us in proper perspective: we only exist because God wants us to (v. 11). Even the way that we are made—the way our bodies are constructed and put together—is according to what He has willed (1 Cor. 12:18). Our existence, like everything God does, is according to the *counsel of His will* (Eph. 1:11).

In the context of Revelation 4:11, our existence by the will of God reminds us that He alone deserves all glory, honor, and power. Planet earth began with Him. Humankind commenced with Him. Everything in this universe will come to a screeching halt because of Him. And all of mankind will give answer to Him and bow before His Son, whom He has appointed the One Man to judge the world (Acts 17:31).

Your life is not about you. My life is not about me. I exist for Him, for His glory, for His honor, to accomplish His purposes, as a testimony to His power.

Too often, our view of life is a spiritual reversal of the Copernican Revolution. We want to think that somehow our life is the central pivot of it all, much like the ancients viewed the earth as the center of the universe. Both are patently false. We must purge from our thinking any humanistic notions that somehow our lives are all about our comfort, pleasure, security, advancement, and ambitions. It is only when you and I put God's glory, honor, and power at the center that everything else in life can possibly fall into place. Buddhism's pessimism, Hinduism's fatalism, and Islam's despotism provide no satisfying answers. Only genuine Christianity offers a workable explanation for the tragedies and enigmas that dog life in a fallen world. The God who willed it all is working to piece it all back together; and when you submit to His will, your life becomes an instrument to proclaim His excellencies (I Peter 2:9; ESV).

(3) God wills your and my eternal salvation.

God willed Christ's sacrifice on the cross to rescue us from this evil age (Gal. 1:4; cf. Acts 2:23; 4:28). He wishes the conversion of every man (Matt. 18:14; 1 Tim. 2:4; 2 Peter 3:9). In an even more specific sense, He willed *your* regeneration (John 1:13; James 1:18).[26] He willed your adoption as sons (Eph. 1:5). Christ willed to reveal the Father to you (Matt. 11:27), and it is the Father's will that Christ keep you and not lose any who have come to Him (John 6:39-40). God's will, not yours, keeps you safe in His hands (10:29)!

(4) God wills to give you a spiritual gift according to what He planned for you and how He wanted you to serve in the body of Christ.

Every believer receives a spiritual gift when he or she becomes (at conversion) a member of the body of Christ. Specifically, the Holy Spirit gives gifts to each believer *as He wills* (1 Cor. 12:11). The specific spiritual gift He gave you was not based on your desire but His. It was based on how He wanted you to serve in the body of Christ.

As you read this book, you will glean the fact that my wife and I live and minister in the Philippines. One of the things I like doing whenever we are back in the States on furlough is visiting the ice cream aisle in the grocery store. I enjoy looking through all the available brands, flavors, and options. And I love exercising the power to choose.

However, spiritual gifts do not work this way. You do not go down the spiritual gifts aisle and choose which gifts you would like to exercise in the body of Christ and how you want to use them. God did that. The gift that you have reflects His choice for you. Rest assured that it is an excellent choice and the same you would have made if you had access to His omniscience. He who willed you into existence and willed your eternal salvation surely knows how you will best fit into His overarching purposes for the body of Christ.

Obviously, since God has given you a spiritual gift, it is His will that you use that spiritual gift for the good of the church (1 Cor. 12:7).

Have you ever given a gift to someone and then worked up the courage to ask how they liked it? Or maybe you did not need to ask because you discovered it one day at the local Goodwill.

For you to have a God-willed spiritual gift and to not be using it is an insult to the God who gave it to you.

(5) God wills that we conduct ourselves honorably and submissively even in a pagan world.

God wills that we keep our conduct honorable by abstaining from fleshly desires and by submitting to our governmental authorities. Such behavior will bring glory to God, as onlookers see our good deeds, and *put to silence the ignorance of foolish men* (1 Peter 2:15). Sometimes we are so focused on what we want—often, frankly, out of selfish motives—that we forget that a good testimony is God's will. Is God more pleased when we manipulate a good deal or when we transact business fairly?

Proverbs confronts head-on the deceitful buyer who plays loose with the facts in order for him to get a good deal.

"It is good for nothing," cries the buyer; But when he has gone his way, then he boasts (20:14).

Years ago, I was traveling in a part of Manila far from my home and needed to take a tricycle to my next destination. (A tricycle is a motorcycle with a sidecar. It is a very common kind of "Point A" to "Point B" short-distance transportation.) I honestly did not know the correct fare, but thought I had a fairly good idea of how much it would normally cost. When the tricycle driver opted to charge me what I thought was an unfair price, I proceeded to haggle with him. Haggling is acceptable in Filipino culture, but there is a line that you should not cross. Evidently I crossed that line because in his anger at me, he spit on the ground in disgust. I walked away from that situation with a heavy heart. I had quibbled over a few pesos and lost something infinitely more important—a God-honoring testimony.

Scripture nowhere commands us to get the best deal, but it does mandate an honorable walk before a watching world.

Having your conduct honorable among the Gentiles, that when they speak against you as evildoers, they may, by your good works which they observe, glorify God in the day of visitation (1 Peter 2:12).

Do we have the testimony of one who is submissive to God-given authorities? This also is God's will (vv. 13-14). We are not to obey authorities when they agree with us or because they are perfect. We obey authorities because God is perfect, and the powers that be have been appointed by Him (Rom. 13:1). Your authority figures are the scaffolding God is using to work on you and to show a pagan world what a supernaturally empowered life looks like.

(6) God wills for men to model His concern for mankind by praying always, everywhere, for everyone.

*I desire therefore that the **men** pray everywhere, lifting up holy hands, without wrath and doubting* (1 Tim. 2:8).

Paul, in expressing his desire for men in the church, is actually expressing God's. God wills that men be *praying* men. We are to pray for all men, especially those in authority. We are to pray for all men so that we will enjoy the necessary "environment" (a) to more ably live a quiet life of godliness and reverence and (b) to see the gospel go forward. We are to share God's heart to see all men come to the knowledge of the truth (vv. 3-7). If that is God's heart, then men should pray everywhere! More prayer in more places by more men means more peace, more freedom to live godly, and more inroads for the gospel.

But how we live as men affects our ability to pray. We are to lift up *holy hands*. We live in a filthy world in which we must constantly battle to maintain our personal holiness. Perhaps a guilty conscience over our *dirty hands* is part of what keeps us men out of prayer meetings!

We must also avoid *anger or quarreling* (v. 8; ESV). Such behavior often produces talk that is hurtful and that grieves the Spirit of God.

Let no corrupt word proceed out of your mouth, but what is good for necessary edification, that it may impart grace to the hearers. And do not grieve the Holy Spirit of God, by whom you were sealed for the day of redemption (Eph. 4:29-30).

Before we can pray effectively, we must mend our strained relationships and forgive those who may have wronged us.

Therefore if you bring your gift to the altar, and there remember that your brother has something against you, leave your gift there before the altar, and go your way. First be reconciled to your brother, and then come and offer your gift (Matt. 5:23-24).

Interestingly, culture castigates or belittles praying as women's work, but *men*, with all their native self-sufficiency, strength, and independence, are the ones that God urges to pray. Prayer on the part of the male elders of the church can heal the sick (James 5:15). Elijah, a man, is the illustration James sets before us to convince us that *the effective, fervent prayer of a righteous man avails much* (James 5:16b).

Is not this call for men to pray a good test of how serious we are about planning our life God's way? We want God's blessing so we can get the car we dream of, the job we covet, or the girl we cannot live without; but we cannot find the time to make it to prayer meeting.

Really?

That kind of "spirituality" is mere posturing, an attempt to use our relationship with God to get what *we* want out of life!

Let me address men directly here. As a gender, we would have a lot more time for prayer if we set aside some of our childish and even harmful time-wasters. One of the biggest time-wasters for men is the current gaming binge. Men are drawn into gaming far more than women are. I asked a former gaming addict one time about this phenomenon, and he explained to me why. Men crave success. Online gaming allows men who are haunted by failure in real life to experience virtual success. It is, in a sense, the ultimate cave-in to passivity: I can live virtually the life that has flopped in reality.

What if men were to devote that time praying? What if, instead of caving in to the passivity of despair, they were to take their burdens and frustrations to the Lord in prayer? They just might find their footing in life! They might regain control of the life that they sense is spinning out of their control. No wonder Satan will throw every hurdle in the way of a man who makes a resolution to pray!

As missionaries, God has blessed us with prayer warriors from one coast of the United States to the other. I would say the majority of those who have expressed their regular practice of praying for us are ladies. But I am thankful for the men who also hold us up faithfully before the throne of grace. One time, we visited a small church where an older man came in for the afternoon service. The pastor told me quietly after the service, "This man is one of your chief prayer warriors." I made it a point to meet him. As we talked, he opened up to me and revealed how God had used a sermon in his life years earlier to burden him to pray. At the time he listened to the sermon, he confessed, he was only praying about an hour a day. He now has 12,000 names or requests on his prayer list. Prayer has become more than a habit to him; it is his life.

(7) God wills for women to be modest, appropriate, and reserved (submissive); and to prioritize, when given the opportunity, marriage and children.

God wills for women in the church to be appropriate, modest, and careful[27] in their dress (1 Tim. 2:9-12). This is anti-cultural. Every billboard, TV commercial, and internet ad tells a woman that she needs to dress in a way that flaunts her body. After all, this is the way to attract the man of her dreams.

God's revealed will is different. Women are to exhibit a submissive demeanor, be willing to listen and learn, and to ever exalt their role of being a wife and mother if given that privilege (5:14). After all, it is in the context of her rearing of children that she will thrive and prosper (2:15).[28]

We are always quick to interject exceptions. What about Queen Esther? What about Judge Deborah? What about the Proverbs 31 woman who transacted business? What about Lydia, the seller of purple? But let's not blunt what God has said!

God is certainly not forbidding work outside the home for a woman or the pursuit of a meaningful career, but He is definitely suggesting where her focus ought to be. Our modern context rejects this as outdated, but listen again to the words God has revealed:

> *In like manner also, that the women adorn themselves in modest apparel, with propriety and moderation, not with braided hair or gold or pearls or costly clothing, but, which is proper for women professing godliness, with good works. Let a woman learn in silence with all submission. And I do not permit a woman to teach or to have authority over a man, but to be in silence. For Adam was formed first, then Eve. And Adam was not deceived, but the woman being deceived, fell into transgression. Nevertheless she will be saved [i.e., thrive and prosper] in childbearing if they continue in faith, love, and holiness, with self-control* (1 Tim. 2:9-15).

My wife and I once met a woman who was working at an insurance office. We asked politely about her family, and she volunteered the fact that she had twin babies. When we inquired about child care, her answer was as honest as it was disconcerting: taking care of twin babies was exhausting and frustrating, so she chose to work instead. It was not for the money. In fact, she confessed to us, her total salary was less than the monthly child care that working forced her to pay. She actually ended up paying for the privilege of working away from her troublesome babies.

(8) God wills that sometimes we suffer for doing right.

Because we work and live in a pagan world, we will experience persecution if we choose to live like a Christian. (Persecution for doing right is as old as Cain and Abel.) First Peter urges us to arm ourselves with the willingness to suffer for what is right.

Therefore, since Christ suffered for us in the flesh, arm yourselves also with the same mind… (1 Peter 4:1a).

Sometimes God wills for us to suffer for our Christian convictions, beliefs, and testimony. How willing are we to face governmental, social, familial, economic, or professional persecution for the sake of His name?

Therefore let those who suffer according to the will of God commit their souls to Him in doing good, as to a faithful Creator (v. 19).

Like a deer caught in the headlights, we are frighteningly caught in our culture's head-over-heels assault on biblical morals. It is only a matter of time before we will suffer for being a Christian, even in the "land of the free and the home of the brave," in the country where coins are still minted with the words "one nation under God." Some have, in fact, already experienced financial loss, social ridicule, and penal consequences for following their Christian convictions.

Many believers in countries where Christians are in the minority understand the suffering they will face if they embrace Jesus, but they bravely do so anyway. My wife and I spent the summer of 2003 ministering in Cambodia. One Wednesday night during our midweek prayer service, the local believers related to us the persecution they had faced since they had turned their back on Buddhism and become followers of Jesus Christ. As their tales of woe mounted in number, I finally asked, "If life as a believer is so challenging, why don't you just go back to being Buddhist?" Their answer startled but pleased me. "Because we found in Jesus forgiveness of sin."

Many Chinese believers have a great burden to take the gospel to the unreached parts of the world that lie between China and Jerusalem. In the book *Back to Jerusalem,* the author tells of the Chinese church's willingness to suffer for the gospel and their preparation for doing so. Headed clandestinely for countries where proselytizing in Jesus' name is illegal, some have studied how to escape from handcuffs and how to jump out of two-story buildings.[29] Why? They are ready to take the gospel to the ends of the earth and are willing to face the suffering it will require.

Even Jesus Himself recognized that not all of the messengers He sends out in His name will return home safely; some will be killed, but He still sends them (Matt. 23:34). When He prepared His disciples for one of their first missions in His name, His lengthiest comments addressed the persecution they would face (10:16-42).

(9) God wills that you live a sexually pure life.

When Paul writes to the Thessalonian believers, he calls them to a life of sanctification. The sanctification which he enjoins upon them relates specifically to sexual purity. He develops three aspects of being sexually pure, all of which have immediate applicability to believers today.

First, we must avoid any kind of sexual immorality (v. 3).

For this is the will of God, your sanctification: that you should abstain from sexual immorality (1 Thess. 4:3).

Sexual immorality is a general term (sometimes translated *fornication*) for any kind of sexual activity that lies outside the bounds of a marriage between one man and one woman. It is sometimes listed with other terms, such as *uncleanness* (moral filthiness or corruption) and *lewdness* (no moral self-control or self-constraint). Scripture is clear that all such activity is a sin against the body and corrupts the Temple of the Lord.

Flee sexual immorality. Every sin that a man does is outside the body, but he who commits sexual immorality sins against his own body. Or do you not know that your body is the temple of the Holy Spirit who is in you, whom you have from God, and you are not your own? (1 Cor. 6:18-19).

Second, we are to control our bodily desires.

...that each of you should know how to possess his own vessel in sanctification and honor, not in passion of lust, like the Gentiles who do not know God (1 Thess. 4:4-5).

We are to do so in a way that communicates our dedication to God ("sanctification") and maintains respectability ("honor"). Do not blame your culture for your failures, as if somehow morals today are worse than they have ever been. God assumes a sexually-driven culture (v. 5); He knows we will be swimming alone against the current.

Remember, only marriage (definitely not "friendship with privileges," shacking up, or pornography) is the God-given provision to satisfy our bodily desires. Anything outside of marriage that we do or watch or read or listen to or touch that stimulates our bodily desires violates God's revealed will!

Third, we are not to defraud, cheat, or take advantage of others sexually.

...that no one should take advantage of and defraud his brother in this matter, because the Lord is the avenger of all such, as we also forewarned you and testified (4:6).

We must not only control our own bodies but live in a way that helps others maintain their purity, holiness, and respectability as God's Temple. What if you do not cross the line sexually, but your actions cause someone else to? In God's eyes, this is not a light matter, and He directly punishes all those who take advantage of or defraud others in this way.

In short, it is God's will that we be sexually pure. Sexual impurity in whatever form or amount compromises our consecration to God and prevents our being useful for anything sacred.

Once again we see that God's will, more than what I do, is who I am. Am I sexually pure? Am I helping others to be sexually pure by my actions? Am I entertaining myself purely? How sincere am I about wanting God's will for my life if I am not pursuing the bodily sanctification that He prizes so highly?

Your marriage, by the way, is the key to your sexual purity. The devil does everything he can before marriage to get two people in bed together, and after marriage he works overtime to keep those same two people out of bed together.[30] Satan will do whatever he can to break up the purity and enjoyment of a marriage.

(10) God wills that you live a thankful life.

Nobody likes people who murmur and complain. Have you ever been around a cranky child? Nothing will drive a parent crazier than listening to and tolerating whining in their children.

God does not like complaining either. It is, in fact, His will that we give thanks for all things. The godly commentator and Presbyterian pastor, Matthew Henry, records in his diary how one night, a little over a year before his death, he was robbed by four men as he was coming home from an evening lecture. He then remarks (in his diary), "What reason have I to be thankful to God, who have travelled so much, and yet was never robbed before."[31] Henry, astonishingly, gives thanks because it was the first time in his entire life that he had been robbed! He had learned to *give thanks in all circumstances* (1 Thess. 5:18; ESV).

God commands us to do everything *without complaining and disputing* (Phil. 2:14). Why? Complaining is a criticism against God. It is a

72

critique of His wisdom or His love or His justice because He is the One who is at work in your circumstances *to will and to do for His good pleasure* (2:13). When we complain, we are criticizing the way God is working out our salvation. For me to be in God's will, I must realize that He is at work through **all** my circumstances (perhaps especially the ones I do not like) conforming me to the image of His Son. I must therefore respond in meekness and thankfulness, knowing that He only gives *good* and *perfect* gifts (James 1:17).

I must be content with my "lot" in life, as Ecclesiastes reminds us.

*So I saw that there is nothing better than that a man should rejoice in his work, for that is his **lot**. Who can bring him to see what will be after him* (3:22; ESV)?

*Behold, what I have seen to be good and fitting is to eat and drink and find enjoyment in all the toil with which one toils under the sun the few days of his life that God has given him, for this is his **lot**. Everyone also to whom God has given wealth and possessions and power to enjoy them, and to accept his **lot** and rejoice in his toil-- this is the gift of God* (5:18-19; ESV).

*Live joyfully with the wife whom you love all the days of your vain life which He has given you under the sun, all your days of vanity; for that is your **portion** in life, and in the labor which you perform under the sun* (9:9).

Too many adults are like children at a birthday party, who spot the biggest piece of cake on the table and wish secretly that the hostess will give it to them. Inevitably, it goes to one of their friends! We, as adults, often feel the same way—like God has handed the best or the biggest or the nicest or the richest to those around us and has given us the most miserable of portions.

BE A PERSON OF THE BOOK!

This chapter has taken us back to the fundamentals of God's revealed will. Frankly, these things are the true litmus test of whether we really want God's will. What more do we expect to know from God when we refuse to study, treasure, meditate on, and obey what He has already willed for us to do? Do we truly want God, His will, His way, His kingdom, and His righteousness? Or is He just a "magic 8-Ball we shake up and peer into whenever we have a decision to make."[32] Too often, we do not really want God and His will. We just want His help to make decisions or bail us out of trouble. We follow Him just enough to ensure that he will let us live our lives in a peaceful pursuit of our own choosing. Such thinking is "nonsense up with which we cannot put"![33]

Rather, we need to remind ourselves that the Christian men and women whom we look up to as heroes were all men and women of the Book. They were people who got the fundamentals down.

We admire, for example, George Müller because it seems that he received whatever he prayed for. Wouldn't it be nice to be able to do that? We overlook the fact that he read his Bible through two hundred times during his lifetime!

Or consider Mary Slessor, the red-headed Scottish missionary to Africa. Her courage and pluck as a single woman missionary in some of the harshest of climates and contexts is almost unbelievable until one sees a picture of her Bible. Nearly every page is filled with her hand-written comments. (The image on the next page is of Mark 8-9 from her Bible.)

We could multiply the names of other "great" Christians—from Matthew Henry to Charles Spurgeon. Like Job, they all highly esteemed God's Words.

I have not departed from the commandment of His lips; I have treasured the words of His mouth more than my necessary food (Job 23:12).

… Only when we are living those things that God has clearly revealed to be His will are we ready to seek further applications of God's Word that seem to have more relevance to our immediate circumstances.

A page of Mary Slessor's Bible (open to the Gospel of Mark)

Used with permission of the Centre for the Study of World Christianity at The University of Edinburgh, File # GB 237 CSWC47/LS2/34.

‹ 6 ›

Light Your Pathway with Scripture

Your testimonies also are my delight and my counselors (Psa. 119:24)

My parents lived on a tight budget and had very little money to spend on cars. The result was that many of our cars were worse than hand-me-downs. One orange Plymouth Volare sticks out in my memory. To say it was orange is actually flattery, given the amount of rust it had. Wire, tape, twine—I forget what all—held various parts under the hood in place. My sister and I were so embarrassed to be seen in it that we would slump down in our seats below the window level. Such cars provided unwanted but ample opportunities for my father to hone his mechanic skills, and I was often called in to help. One of my primary jobs was to hold the light while my father repaired the latest malfunction. The challenge was to hold the light correctly so that it did not shine in his eyes but rather on the place he wanted it.

The Psalms uses the imagery of light to describe God Word: *Your word is a lamp to my feet and a light to my path* (Psa. 119:105). Virtually any Christian would embrace the sentiments of this verse, but we all struggle with how to shine the light of the Word on our pathway correctly. After all, the Bible is a big book with 1189 chapters, over 3100 verses, and about 770,000 words (in the New King James Version).

Once you have aligned yourself with the clearly revealed will of God—the explicit directives we looked at in the previous chapter—how do you move on to make real-time application of the Bible to your immediate circumstances?

Where does the Bible tell you, for instance, what to choose as a major in college? Where to live? Or what mutual fund to invest in? How would you know, for example, whether you should buy a home or continue renting? Should you buy a 1998 Ford E-250 van or splurge on a 2017 Mustang? Should you marry Margaret or Matilda? Accept a proposal from Burt or Bob?

Does it even matter? Should you even seek guidance from God about such personal, individualized matters?

We cannot answer all these questions in this chapter, but we will look at some practical ideas for applying Scripture to our everyday decisions. Let us first consider two wrong ways of shining the light of Scripture on our decisions.

WRONG METHODS OF USING SCRIPTURE

(1) Randomly opening Scripture

You have probably heard the overworked anecdote of the man who randomly opened the Bible to seek guidance and landed on Matthew 27:5: *And Judas went and hanged himself.* He could not immediately put his finger on just how to apply it to himself so he thought he would try a second time. He alighted on Luke 10:37: *Go, and do thou likewise* (KJV). Half convinced of the grim duty lying before him, he decided to try again and discern God's timetable for his unfortunate fate. He landed on John 13:27: *That thou doest, do quickly* (KJV).

Actually, there is some truth behind this anecdote. Good and godly men of the past often randomly opened Scripture in order to discover the Lord's will. Count Zinzendorf and the Moravians practiced it regularly. They called it "consulting the oracle." The weighty decision of who would be the first among the Moravians to serve as missionaries in the West Indies was decided, in part, by consulting the oracle.

The Wesley brothers, John and Charles, also believed in consulting the oracle. When he was fifty-one years of age, John Wesley was so weak physically and so sure he was going to die shortly that he wrote the epitaph for his own gravestone. This fear of an early death was confirmed "Scripturally." Wesley consulted the Bible four times randomly and "each time the verse he lighted upon referred to death or suffering."[34]

When he told the Fetter Lane Society, his brother Charles would not believe that this word from the Lord was true, so he consulted the oracle himself and lighted upon Ezekiel 24:16: *Son of man, behold, I take from thee the desire of thine eyes with a stroke: yet neither shalt thou mourn nor weep, neither shall thy tears run down* (KJV).

Charles became convinced. Ezekiel had stated it clearly: his beloved brother, the desire of his eyes, would die. Fortunately, John Wesley recovered from his illness and went on to live over thirty-five more years, dying in his upper eighties.

(2) Appropriating verses that do not apply to your situation

In shining the light of Scripture on our pathway, we must not assume that every passage speaks directly to our situation. It does not. Not every command in the Bible applies to us. Neither does every promise.

Take the verse from Ezekiel that Charles' finger happened upon in our story above. Yes, the verse is speaking of death, but it is speaking specifically of the death of Ezekiel's wife, not Charles' brother.

This problem of misappropriating verses when hunting for God's guidance is at least as old as John Newton who, when agonizing over whether to leave his current pastorate and accept the call to another, found help in God's statement to Paul in the book of Acts: *For I am with you, and no one will attack you to hurt you; for I have many people in this city* (18:10).

Upon further reflection, Newton realized that he was not Paul and his new pastorate would not be in Corinth.[35]

How many times has Jeremiah 29:11 been misappropriated by young men groping for a promise that a certain girl who has caught their attention is the "one" for them?

For I know the thoughts that I think toward you, says the LORD, thoughts of peace and not of evil, to give you a future and a hope.

What could be clearer? *Peace... a future* (that obviously includes her)! However, verse 10 provides the context for verse 11: *When seventy years are completed for Babylon.* Verse 11 is explaining the why behind God's promise of deliverance from Babylon after the seventy-year Captivity. It is not promising that your current relationship will come to the expected end of a marriage altar, complete with flowers, organ music, and a beautiful bride.

Does Jeremiah 29:11 have any relevance for a believer today? Absolutely! But not by direct application to our immediate situation.[36] We must begin by extracting from the verse the truth it is teaching us about God. In this case, we could state it something like this: "God does not work to destroy His people through times of chastisement." We would then meditate prayerfully on that principle to see how the Holy Spirit might make application to our immediate circumstances.

For example, you might be under God's hand of chastisement and need the comfort of knowing that God's purpose in disciplining His people does not include destroying them or grinding them into the gravel until they grovel. His chastisements come to an end once they have accomplished His purposes; restoration then follows.

Another easily misapplied passage is Isaiah 54:11-13:

> *O you afflicted one, tossed with tempest, and not comforted, behold, I will lay your stones with colorful gems, and lay your foundations with sapphires. I will make your pinnacles of rubies, your gates of crystal, and all your walls of precious stones. All your children shall be taught by the LORD, and great shall be the peace of your children.*

What a wonderful promise, a person could argue, of how God will restore my troubled family and give me a peaceful relationship with my children! Unfortunately, the verse applies to the city of Jerusalem and to her children. It is a reminder that the God who makes promises keeps them, but this promise speaks specifically of the restoration of Jerusalem.

We could multiply examples of this kind of misapplication of God's Word. I am tempted here to propose a new hermeneutical rule. Here goes: "When fishing for a direct word from the Lord (perhaps especially in the Old Testament prophets), be careful to catch something that you can legitimately use."

The temptation, of course, is to coerce a passage you "catch" to address a situation that it does not fit. God can and does speak to us through His Word, but we need to make sure we have accurately understood a passage's context and meaning rather than zero in on wording that matches (coincidentally) our particular circumstance.

There are several dangers in misapplying God's Word, but one of the worst is a sense that God has let you down. Too many people's spiritual lives have been damaged because they feel like God "gave" them some verse, and they claimed it; but then God did not live up to what He had promised them. They fault God when they should instead fault themselves for failing to understand what the passage they claimed really meant.

RIGHT METHODS OF USING SCRIPTURE IN DECISION-MAKING

As we make decisions, we need to shine the light of God's Word on our pathway, but we must do so correctly. I have personally found it helpful to run my decisions through Scripture by using a fivefold grid, which I have delineated below. The grid moves from that which is most objective to that which is more subjective.

(1) Clear (and relevant) commands

When you face a decision, first think through commands of Scripture that have clear relevance to your decision (or circumstance).

A clear command of Scripture prompted the Eleven to replace Judas and bring their total back to twelve.

For it is written in the book of Psalms: 'Let his dwelling place be desolate, And let no one live in it'; and, **'Let another take his office.'** *Therefore, of these men who have accompanied us all the time that the Lord Jesus went in and out among us . . .* (Acts 1:20-21).

In the same way, look for clear commands of God that address your situation. Where God gives a clear command, the decision is already made for you. (Remember . . . It is always God's will that we do His will.)

Ready for an assignment?

Match the following clear commands with those situations in your life to which they might have immediate application:

  ⇨ *Do not be unequally yoked together with unbelievers. For what fellowship has righteousness with lawlessness? And what communion has light with darkness* (2 Cor. 6:14)?

  ⇨ *Render therefore to all their due: taxes to whom taxes are due, customs to whom customs, fear to whom fear, honor to whom honor* (Rom. 13:7).

- *Owe no one anything except to love one another, for he who loves another has fulfilled the law* (Rom. 13:8).

- *For even when we were with you, we commanded you this: If anyone will not work, neither shall he eat. For we hear that there are some who walk among you in a disorderly manner, not working at all, but are busybodies. Now those who are such we command and exhort through our Lord Jesus Christ that they work in quietness and eat their own bread* (2 Thess. 3:10-12).

- *Wives, submit to your own husbands, as to the Lord* (Eph. 5:22).

- *Husbands, love your wives, just as Christ also loved the church and gave Himself for her* (v. 25).

- *You shall have no other gods before Me* (Exod. 20:3).

- *Jesus said to him, "'You shall love the LORD your God with all your heart, with all your soul, and with all your mind.' This is the first and great commandment. And the second is like it: 'You shall love your neighbor as yourself'"* (Matt. 22:37-39).

The list could go on and on, but surely you can see how these commands could have very relevant application to business decisions, relationship issues, tax season, or establishing life priorities.

You will also notice that the commands I have chosen above are those that are universally applicable. That is, they are always true, regardless of the time or place. I did not, for example, choose time- or person-specific commands, such as the following:

- *Jesus said to her, "Go, call your husband, and come here"* (John 4:16).

- *So when He saw them, He said to them, "Go, show yourselves to the priests." And so it was that as they went, they were cleansed* (Luke 17:14).

- *Then Nathan said to the king, "Go, do all that is in your heart, for the LORD is with you"* (2 Sam. 7:3).

These directives address specific individuals at specific times in their lives. They could have application, if you draw valid principles from the overall context, but you should not see in them some kind of immediate word from God to fetch your husband, start a ministry to Jewish families with the last name of Cohen, or go out on the limb financially and buy that 2017 Mustang you are drooling over. Surely we can see the nonsense in practicing this kind of illegitimate immediate application.

As you can see, there are numerous relevant commands in Scripture, which can shed very helpful light on your pathway, if you will take the time to think through them when facing decisions, crises, or crossroads.

(2) Passages that specifically address situations (decisions) like yours

Rather than go "fishing" somewhere in Isaiah or Jeremiah for obscure promises of comfort, look up passages that relate exactly or closely to your specific situation. Consider the following examples:

Your situation: God has given you wonderful children, but discipline issues are frustrating you. How should you discipline children? For what should you discipline them? What should you use in disciplining them?

Relevant passages: Proverbs includes several passages intended to impart wisdom to those disciplining children (3:12; 13:24; 19:18; 22:15; 23:13-14; 29:15, 17). Base your child-rearing decisions on a careful study of those passages.

Your situation: Your spending is out of control. Poor financial decisions are bleeding you dry. In addition, retirement is looming, and you increasingly sense the need to make financial provision for the future. Where can you turn in the Bible for help?

Relevant passages: Go through Proverbs with a colored pencil or highlighter and mark all those verses that relate to wealth, work, and business. Filling your mind with these passages will provide a chiropractic-like adjustment of your spending habits and even your financial priorities.

These verses will not help you, though, if you do not apply and live them. A friend of ours has attended Dave Ramsey seminars two or three times but is still mired in major financial trouble. In counseling him, I challenged him to make a budget and live within his income. He admitted frankly that he had never done anything like that. He enjoys listening to Dave Ramsey, even sees the wisdom of his advice, but does not have the discipline to follow through. As we study what the Bible says about our decisions, we need to remember James' wise words of counsel: *Be doers of the word, and not hearers only, deceiving yourselves* (1:22).

Your situation: You are reaching marriageable age and are wanting to know some specifics about the kind of woman to look for in a wife. Is there any chapter in the Bible that sets forth admirable qualities in a woman?

Relevant passages: Work through Proverbs 31 (vv. 10-31), the portrait of an exemplary wife and mother. That is the kind of woman you want to find and marry!

Your situation: As a pastor, you are concerned for the growth and unity of your church. You have crisscrossed America attending seminars that you hoped would provide the "secret" to growing your church but to no seeming avail. Is there any extended passage in Scripture that addresses how to encourage a church to walk in unity? Any passage that provides instruction for a church and its minister?

Relevant passages: Do a serious study of Ephesians 4:1-16, the longest passage in the New Testament on church maturity and unity, or of 1 Timothy, a manual for ministers' personal and church life. Careful meditation and genuine Spirit-led application of these passages would surely bear fruit in your ministry.

Your situation: Your husband is unsaved, and you face the constant juggling act of pleasing God or obeying your husband. Has God included any passage in His Word that gives advice to women living with unsaved husbands?

Relevant passages: Memorize I Peter 3:1-6, and ask the Spirit of God to make appropriate application of that passage to your marriage. Your prayerful meditation of that passage will do more to calm your fears and direct your steps than hours of talking with your girlfriends about it.

Your situation: You have changed so radically since you became a Christian that you are facing ridicule and harassment from friends and relatives. You no longer feel comfortable at family reunions or similar gatherings because of the raucous drinking and worldly entertainment. Is there anything in the Bible written to help Christians living in a world hostile to their faith?

Relevant passages: Hopefully, you guessed I Peter—the entire book provides help to newer believers who are facing persecution because of their faith in Jesus.

Your situation: You are having doubts about your salvation. You have genuinely (to the best of your ability) professed faith in Christ but questions still linger: do I really have eternal life?

Relevant passages: Ever thought about working through the book of 1 John? After all, ministering assurance is its author's stated purpose: *These things I have written to you who believe in the name of the Son of God, that you may know that you have eternal life, and that you may continue to believe in the name of the Son of God* (5:13).

The last two examples above show that there are whole books in Scripture that discuss specific topics, tackle certain doctrines, or sort through common problems. A good study Bible or basic commentary will give the principal theme of each book of the Bible (usually in the introductory material to that book). That principal theme tells you

when to use that book in your life. God has given His Words to light your pathway. Shine them on it!

Are you facing unexplained suffering? Pondering the claims of Jesus? Curious about what lies ahead in the future? Scan through the themes of the books of the Bible until you find the one most appropriate to the questions uppermost in your mind.

In other words, fish for help in those books that most closely match your circumstances, not in remote oracles completely detached from your situation. You don't fish for tuna in your cow pond or for freshwater catfish in the South China Sea!

(3) Biblical characters (good and bad) in life circumstances comparable to yours

Learn from the people you find in Scripture, especially those in life circumstances similar to yours. Admittedly, studying the lives of people in the Bible can be a bit tricky because it is not as if God's directives for them are automatically His directives for you. For example, reading Genesis 22 should not convince you to sacrifice your favorite child on Mount McKinley or Kilimanjaro!

Begin by looking for a person whose life (in Scripture) matches the situation you are in, models the behavior you desire, or resembles your personality. Then, study the person's life. Do not focus merely on their responses. Bring God into the picture. What was God teaching that person through their circumstances, personality, or responses? Our goal is not to mimic the person's morals but to better understand the God who oversaw their circumstances and is superintending yours.

Perhaps it is not the entire person's life but just one episode of his or her life that matches yours. Study that episode (although studying first the person's life as a whole may better enable you to evaluate what God was doing in the one episode that you have zeroed in on). Find the key principle that God was teaching them. Again, do not just state it as a moral. State it as a God-centered principle. I sometimes advise my students to make it a sentence that has God as the subject. Your goal is to learn about the God who saw them through circumstances similar to yours. The details of their life will probably be far different than those in yours, but God's relational dealings with them and the lessons He was teaching them may be remarkably parallel to what He wants to teach you.

Think of Daniel, for example. Would you not agree that courage characterizes his actions in Daniel 1? It would be easy to come up with a winsome slogan like "Act with courage" or "Remain loyal under pressure" as an appropriate summary of that episode in his life. Better far, however, would be to bring God into the picture. Daniel's courage stemmed from his desire to honor God. God, in turn, honored Daniel. I summarize Daniel 1 as follows: *God honors those who honor Him* (a rephrasing of 1 Sam. 2:30). This gives you a God-centered principle that you can then apply to your life when you face pressures to compromise your faith or Christian testimony.

When approached from this angle, your study of people in Scripture—especially those in similar situations to yours—will be extremely beneficial. You will find committed Christian men who had serious disagreements (Paul and Barnabas), women who could not have children (Hannah and Elizabeth), wives whose husbands put them in difficult situations (Sarah and Michal), teenagers torn from their families and thrust into foreign settings (Joseph and Daniel), and leaders who sinned greatly (King Saul, King David, and Peter). God intends us to study the lives of these biblical characters and learn from them.

Now all these things happened to them as examples, and they were written for our admonition, upon whom the ends of the ages have come (1 Cor. 10:11).

(4) General principles that should influence your actions

Have you ever been confronted with a statement similar to this? "Show me a chapter and verse that says I cannot do it, and I will stop." Is this valid thinking? Do we really have no guidance from God when it comes to smoking cigarettes, subscribing to Sports Illustrated's swimsuit issue, or excessive online gaming—simply because we have no chapter and verse?

Should not any "wish" of God become to us a supreme command? There is a story (often embellished) about the great confederate general Stonewall Jackson and a visit he paid to his commander, General Robert E. Lee, during adverse weather conditions. A man who accompanied Jackson on the visit describes it this way: "During the winter spent at Moss Neck, General Jackson took me with him to General Lee's headquarters on one occasion when a deep snow was falling. General Lee said he regretted that General Jackson should come out on such a day, whereupon the latter, smiling pleasantly, said: 'I received your note, sir, saying you wished to see me.'"[37] Jackson viewed the wish of his commander as a command—to be obeyed promptly and without regard to personal comfort or safety.

To be sure, we need to be very careful about forcing people into certain actions about which the Bible does not speak clearly. Christian leaders can far too easily bind the consciences of those under them by using passages that have been tortured to make an application that supports *their* wishes.

There is a place, however, for the heart that yearns to know what God "wishes" and has determined to regard them as sacred commands. Our point here is this: give God a chance to speak by applying general biblical principles to your situation. The "show-me-a-chapter-and-verse" argument is typically a cop-out, an attempt to keep a cherished position, not because we genuinely think it is God-honoring, but because we do not want to explore too deeply what God says.

The person who truly values wisdom will want to know what God says and will take the initiative to explore His opinion statements found in His Word. It all boils down to whether we are genuinely striving for the coveted "well done" given to those who precisely handle and doggedly live "the word of truth" (2 Tim. 2:15).

One genre of Scripture particularly challenging and commonly overlooked, found primarily in Exodus 20 to Deuteronomy 34, is that classified as "Old Testament Law." As New Testament Christians, we are no longer under the law but are instead under grace.

Does that render Old Testament Law obsolete, no longer of any value to us as sophisticated denizens of the twenty-first century? I would argue that Old Testament Law still bears witness to the character of God, to His desire for a relationship with His people, and to the attitudes or actions He values in them.

Have you ever dismissed the following verse as irrelevant?

When you reap the harvest of your land, you shall not wholly reap the corners of your field when you reap, nor shall you gather any gleaning from your harvest. You shall leave them for the poor and for the stranger: I am the LORD your God (Lev. 23:22).

Rather than shrug it off, why not consider what it reveals about God's heart for the poor. He cares about their needs and urges His people not to hoard for their own usage **all** that might be rightfully theirs.

Many other passages from the Old Testament would yield similarly fruitful guidance to our (naturally selfish) lives if we would scour them for the insight they give into God's character and the behavior He wishes in His people.

Admittedly much more accessible are the general principles Paul gives in his discussions of disputable matters (Rom. 14:1-15:16; 1 Cor. 8-10). Here are six from 1 Corinthians that I have recast in the form of questions:

Question #1: Does it injure or impair my body's function as God's Temple?

*Flee sexual immorality. Every sin that a man does is outside the body, but he who commits sexual immorality sins against his own **body**. Or do you not know that your **body** is the temple of the Holy Spirit who is in you, whom you have from God, and you are not your own? For you were bought at a price; therefore glorify God in your **body** and in your spirit, which are God's (6:18-20).*

*Do you not know that you are the **temple** of God and that the Spirit of God dwells in you? If anyone defiles the **temple** of God, God will destroy him. For the **temple** of God is holy, which **temple** you are (3:16-17).*

Question #2: Is it truly beneficial for my Christian life?

*All things are lawful for me, but all things are not **helpful**. All things are lawful for me, but I will not be brought under the power of any (6:12).*

*All things are lawful for me, but not all things are **helpful**; all things are lawful for me, but not all things edify (10:23).*

Question #3: Will it build me (or someone else) up spiritually?

*All things are lawful for me, but not all things are helpful; all things are lawful for me, but not all things **edify** (10:23).*

Question #4: Does it give others the right opinion of my God?

*Therefore, whether you eat or drink, or whatever you do, do all to the **glory of God** (10:31).*

Question #5: Will it be a stumbling block to other believers?

*Therefore, if food makes my brother **stumble**, I will never again eat meat, lest I make my brother **stumble** (8:13).*

Question #6: Is it addicting or all-consuming?

*All things are lawful for me, but all things are not helpful. All things are lawful for me, but I will not be brought **under the power** of any (6:12).*

These six questions have wide-ranging application—from sexual purity to what we eat. They also reflect the spirit of a more mature believer. In choosing things that are helpful, non-addicting, and edifying, Paul is admitting that there are other options available to him. *All things are lawful for me.* He is certainly not saying that clearly unbiblical or immoral things are lawful; he is referring to things that we would refer to as "non-moral" or "disputed."

Yet even among these kinds of things, Paul is arguing that a more mature believer will not just indulge because "after all, there's no chapter and verse." Rather he will reflect on those things that are lawful and choose from among them those things that display excellence.

Try applying these principles to smoking cigarettes or chewing tobacco, surfing the internet, watching movies, going into bars, spending time alone in your girlfriend's apartment, online gaming, or frequenting buffet restaurants. (Don't stone me for that last one.) What you will find is that the Word of God is *living and powerful, and sharper than any two-edged sword* (Heb. 4:12).

(5) What God is teaching you in your regular personal time with Him

I have deliberately placed this last because it is the most subjective of the five ways that we can shine God's light on our pathway. Nonetheless, it is a reality, witnessed to by God's people throughout church history and experienced in my own life.

God is so absolutely and completely sovereign that He even guides and works through where we are currently reading in our devotional time. If you are praying over a decision or facing a certain crisis, many times He will lead you (at least in part) through what He is teaching you in your personal time with Him.

My wife comes from a large family with ten children. (She often accuses me of only having half a family since there were only five in mine.) So when it came to having children, she naturally wanted a passel herself. During her first pregnancy everything looked good until about two weeks before her delivery date when the doctor suddenly discovered that the baby was transverse, the umbilical cord was in the wrong place, and we needed an immediate C-section.

That was not a part of *our* plans! C-sections often limit the number of children you can have, and exponentially increase the pain involved and the time of recovery.

We opted to delay the surgery and give ourselves to prayer over the matter. As we prayed, nothing changed. The doctor even tried to turn the baby; our daughter just flipped back into the transverse position. (Some children are stubborn from *before* the day they are born.)

We sought counsel. One piece of advice was for my wife to stand on her head. Have you ever seen a nine-month pregnant woman stand on her head? It would go viral on America's Funniest Home videos!

Eventually we consented to the surgery, with the feeling that we were getting God's second best. What about having all those children we wanted? It weighed heavily on my wife's mind.

The day before surgery, my wife was reading in the Psalms. In the course of her normal reading through Scripture, the Lord neon-highlighted for her the following verse:

As for God, His way is perfect; the word of the LORD is proven; He is a shield to all who trust in Him (18:30).

That Scripture was exactly what my wife needed. God's ways are perfect, and His dealings with us were no exception. She took those words with her into the surgery room.

Ten years and four C-sections later, my wife again became pregnant. We knew we were on the edge, safety-wise. Doctors in the Philippines, where we were at the time, typically allowed only three or, at the most, four C-sections. This pregnancy would have to be her last. After her first ultrasound, my wife walked through the door of our home and burst into tears. "I heard," she informed me, "the heartbeats." She needed to repeat it before I got it—heartbeats, plural. She was carrying twins. God was giving us two precious children for the price of one C-section. More than that, God was proving Psalm 18:30 in her life. What He was doing for her was indeed perfect.

I could multiply examples, but this book is not intended to be an autobiography. You get the point. No doubt if you have walked with God for any length of time, you have experienced the same. God has an uncanny way of dealing with you, comforting you, guiding you, and transforming you through your regular, personal reading of His Word. When you think about the number of days you have skipped your devotional time or skimped on the amount you read or absentmindedly re-read what you read the day before, God's sovereignty in timing the verses we need with the crises we face becomes one of the greatest evidences of divine guidance.

THE BIBLE IS GOD'S MOUTH

The view of the Reformers—articulated, for example, in the 1560 Scottish Confession of Faith authored by John Knox and others—was that the Bible is God's mouth.[38] In some ways, the whole point of this chapter is to suggest practical ways for opening God's mouth and hearing Him speak.

The Bible is, in fact, alive. Far more than a mere collection of old, dead oracles that God gave in the past, it is a book in which God's voice still speaks in the present tense[39]:

*Therefore, as the Holy Spirit **says**: Today, if you will hear His voice* (Heb. 3:7).

*And you have forgotten the exhortation which **speaks** to you as to sons: My son, do not despise the chastening of the LORD, nor be discouraged when you are rebuked by Him* (12:5).

*See that you do not refuse Him who **speaks**. For if they did not escape who refused Him who spoke on earth, much more shall we not escape if we turn away from Him who **speaks** from heaven* (12:25).

‹ 7 ›

Pray for Wisdom

If any of you lacks wisdom, let him ask of God (James 1:5)

We were at the front end of a very busy time of travel in our ministry when my wife's daily-recurring headaches plunged her into a week-long battle with a migraine. Should I cancel an upcoming meeting in order to give my wife rest, or should I push through with our schedule, assuming my wife would improve? Doctors suggested the former; our itinerary dictated the latter. Caught between a rock and a hard place, I took a few minutes one afternoon to lay the matter before the Lord in prayer.

One clear privilege we have when it comes to planning our lives God's way is to pray. All believers agree on the importance of praying for wisdom when placed in situations where we do not know what to do. David did this when confronted with a delicate situation involving the city of Keilah.

> *Then they told David, saying, "Look, the Philistines are fighting against Keilah, and they are robbing the threshing floors." Therefore David inquired of the LORD, saying, "Shall I go and attack these Philistines?" And the LORD said to David, "Go and attack the Philistines, and save*

Keilah." But David's men said to him, "Look, we are afraid here in Judah. How much more then if we go to Keilah against the armies of the Philistines?" Then David inquired of the LORD once again. And the LORD answered him and said, "Arise, go down to Keilah. For I will deliver the Philistines into your hand" (1 Sam. 23:1-4).

Later in the same chapter, David again sought the Lord for wisdom at a time when he was not sure what would happen.

Then Saul called all the people together for war, to go down to Keilah to besiege David and his men. When David knew that Saul plotted evil against him, he said to Abiathar the priest, "Bring the ephod here." Then David said, "O LORD God of Israel, Your servant has certainly heard that Saul seeks to come to Keilah to destroy the city for my sake. "Will the men of Keilah deliver me into his hand? Will Saul come down, as Your servant has heard? O LORD God of Israel, I pray, tell Your servant." And the LORD said, "He will come down." Then David said, "Will the men of Keilah deliver me and my men into the hand of Saul?" And the LORD said, "They will deliver you" (vv. 8-12).

If you put the two sets of verses together, David asked the Lord for direction a total of four times in 1 Samuel 23. All four times, God answered David with a clear affirmative. Have you ever wondered how God communicated His answer? The passage actually tells us: it was the ephod, one of the priestly garments (vv. 6, 9). Bound to the ephod was the breastplate of judgment (Exod. 28:28). The word "judgment" in this context has the idea of a verdict or a decision. Part of the breastplate's function was to serve as a means of "seeking a decision from God" (v. 15; NLT) because in it were placed the Urim and Thummim (v. 30). Not much is known of these two stones; we infer from the available data that they in some way or another indicated the answer to a yes or no question (Num. 27:21; Ezra 2:62-63).

Have you ever wished for these two stones? Wouldn't it be nice to ask God yes or no questions and get clear answers? Should we expect the same today?

Even in the time of Ezra and Nehemiah, no clear way existed to verify the true status of those who claimed to be priests but had no genealogical proof. The decision was made to exclude them until a priest should arise who, once again, had the Urim and Thummim (Ezra 2:63).

Another Old Testament method of receiving a divine verdict was casting lots, perhaps roughly equivalent to the modern practice of drawing straws or flipping a coin. Casting lots correctly identified Jonathan as the guilty eater (1 Sam. 14:42) and Jonah as the storm causer (Jonah 1:7). The Apostolic Eleven even cast lots to determine which of two men was the God-appointed successor to Judas, and they viewed the result as divinely given (Acts 1:26). Impious Roman soldiers, ironically, cast lots for Jesus' clothing (John 19:24).

What are we supposed to do as New Testament believers? Should we ask God yes and no questions and expect some kind of clear affirmative? Or should we prayerfully cast lots as some well-meaning believers have done? How are we supposed to pray when we do not know what to do?

DIVINE GUIDANCE TO THE BEST CHOICE

The Epistle of James answers these (and other) questions by penning these well-known words:

If any of you lacks wisdom, let him ask of God, who gives to all liberally and without reproach, and it will be given to him (1:5).

When we are in a trial and we are not sure what to do or how to approach it, we are to pray for wisdom. Let me repeat that: we are to pray for **wisdom.** (More about the importance of that later.)

James, in fact, encourages us to ask for wisdom **unashamedly**. God is a generous Giver when it comes to wisdom and will not scorn or rebuke you for asking for it. He does not take our crises lightly, nor does He expect us just to shrug our shoulders and hunker down until the calamity passes over. *God is our refuge and strength, a very present help in trouble* (Psa. 46:1).

In addition, James emboldens us to ask for wisdom **expectantly**. God will give wisdom, the verse promises, to those who ask for it.

James does add a condition to the promise, however, by asserting that we need to ask **unreservedly.**

But let him ask in faith, with no doubting, for he who doubts is like a wave of the sea driven and tossed by the wind. For let not that man suppose that he will receive anything from the Lord (James 1:6-7).

The person who doubts is someone who is double minded (v. 8)— they have not fully committed themselves to obeying the wisdom that God will give them, but still have some reservations as to the direction in which they will finally go. A person like that can have no confidence that God will answer his prayer for wisdom.

Now, back to James' directive to pray for **wisdom** and the significance of what he says. Too often, instead of praying for wisdom, we want God to give us a quick "yes" or "no" answer to a decision that is plaguing us. "Lord, should I marry Margaret? Or Matilda? Or is Henrietta actually the right one?"

To ask the Lord "yes" or "no" questions in prayer as we seek His guidance is not wrong. It is unavoidable and is part of our very-privileged dependence on God as our Father. However, I want to remind us that we possess neither Urim nor Thummim. If we jump too quickly in prayer to seeking a yes/no answer, we open ourselves up to impressions. Then . . . too often . . . we rely on those impressions—especially those felt after a time of prayer—as the clearly God-given "yes" or "no" answer to our questions. God wants to teach you something through the search-for-wisdom process, not just beam an impression into your sub-conscious. A prayer for wisdom is a prayer for God to help you come up with the right information so that the wise choice becomes obvious.

I mentioned earlier how my wife's weeklong migraine plunged me into a crisis: do I continue on in our heavy travel schedule or drop everything in order to give her rest? I came out of my time of prayer that afternoon with the firm impression that we should push through with our schedule. Then I talked the matter over with my wife. When I found out exactly where she stood physically, and what she felt like she needed in order to recover, we both agreed it was best not to continue with our schedule, and we canceled one week of our itinerary. The additional information imparted by my wife was what God used to help me make the right decision. I could not properly take care of my wife as a married man ought (1 Cor. 7:33-34a) if we continued at our hectic pace. God answered our prayer for wisdom (even if it did go against my initial impression).

A CAUTION ABOUT IMPRESSIONS AND SIGNS

Remember, we are to pray for **wisdom**, not for an impression. There is a difference. An impression is feeling-based. Impressions can be right or wrong, lasting or transient. Identifying the source of an impression can be tricky.

Evangelist George Whitefield was given in his younger years to uttering "prophecies" based on what he felt were God-given impressions. At the birth of his only son, he named him John because he (prophetically) perceived that his son would become a mighty preacher of righteousness. Sadly, his son died in infancy. Whitefield emerged from the disappointment a wiser man and much more restrained in viewing his impressions as prophecies.

Whitefield's example should caution us about equating our impressions with Spirit-given utterances. We, like him, prefer to equate the two. However, we should be slow to attach the Spirit's signature to our varied notions. We do not want to deny the Holy Spirit a voice in our lives, neither do we want to go to the opposite extreme and hear His voice behind every splendid thought we have.

On a few occasions in the New Testament, the Spirit spoke to believers, but in almost every case it involved a new or special step in the progress of the Gospel—throwing the Gospel net to a proselyte, then a God-fearer, then to Gentiles everywhere (Acts 8:29; 10:19; 13:2, 4). We know nothing as to how He spoke with them, nor are their circumstances completely analogous to ours. Who among us can say that they have been "snatched away" (NET) as Philip was (8:39)?

The primary ongoing work of the Holy Spirit to believers is to reveal Jesus to us through the Word and to conform us more into His image (1 Cor. 2:10-12; 2 Cor. 3:18). Passages that speak of the Spirit leading us refer to His leading us to put to death the desires and deeds of our flesh and to nurture instead His fruit in our lives (Rom. 8:12-14; Gal. 5:16-25).[40]

Much is said about the Spirit and His role in the inspiration of the New Testament. He led the Apostles to remember what they had learned from Jesus, revealed to them more about Jesus, and guided them (infallibly) in the recording of that revelation (John 14:26; 16:13; 1 Cor. 2:13). It stands to reason that He would then primarily (almost exclusively) speak to us from those things He inspired. That is, He *has* spoken (in Scripture) and—through His work of reminding, illuminating, convincing, applying, and convicting—He *still* speaks to us from what He has spoken.

The Spirit will do so by bringing things to our remembrance. That is, He may cause certain thoughts to come into our minds. However, all such "thoughts" must be evaluated as to their true source (not all our thoughts come from the Spirit) and brought into captivity to Christ (2 Cor. 10:5). Examples of where the Spirit may "speak" in this fashion include wooing to salvation, conviction of sin, a call to ministry, help in a time of persecution, and unanticipated redirection (Matt. 10:20; John 16:8; Acts 13:2; 16:6-7; Rev. 22:17).

In summary, I am not denying that the Spirit may lead, nudge, prompt, or place something on our heart.[41] We would probably all agree that the Spirit still ministers to us in ways that we do not fully understand.[42] Rather, I am urging us to stay securely within Scripture's fences and use caution before we automatically assume that an impression (or thought) is from the Holy Spirit.

Similarly, we should be careful about praying for signs or laying out fleeces (like Gideon did). I was at a conference once and the issue of praying for signs came up during a question-and-answer time. An outspoken man toward the back of the auditorium weighed in loudly with these words, *an evil and adulterous generation seeks after a sign* (Matt. 12:39). Everyone knew on which side of the discussion he stood!

Understand, first of all, that there is a difference between asking God for information and for a sign. A request for information enables us to make a wiser decision, whereas a sign can be a request for almost anything. It may or may not be related to the decision at hand. A man could, for example, ask God to make it rain on a summer day in the Sahara Desert as a sign that he should marry a certain woman (but only if he does *not* want to marry her).

Putting out "fleeces," an allusion to Gideon's actions in the book of Judges (6:37-40), results from weak faith. Gideon did not use it to determine the will of the Lord. Gideon himself acknowledged that God had already revealed to him His will: "If you [God] will save Israel by my [Gideon's] hand **as You have said** . . . (Judg. 6:36). Gideon's fleece-laying reveals more about Gideon's doubt-filled disposition than anything else. In fact, he is so weak in faith that once God answers his initial fleece, he lays out a second one and asks God for the reverse of what he asked Him the first time.

Does the Lord answer prayers for signs? Perhaps! If we take Jesus' ministry as our paradigm, He refused signs (essentially) to those who had no heart to believe (Matt. 12:39), while dealing very charitably with those weak in faith—His graciousness, for example, in meeting Thomas' "need" for further confirmation of His resurrection (John 20:27). So He may also respond graciously to our nagging unbelief.

However, most fleece-laying or sign-asking is not an indication of spiritual maturity, but rather the opposite.

KNOWING WHAT IS SPIRITUALLY IMPORTANT

Another passage that connects praying to wisdom and the will of God is Colossians 1:9-12. Understanding its significance begins with a careful reading of verse 9.

> *For this reason we also, since the day we heard it, do not cease to pray for you, and to ask that you may be filled with the knowledge of His will **in all wisdom and spiritual understanding**.*

When we stop our reading partway (even "most-way") through verse 9, contented with the thought that we just need to pray that God would fill us with *the knowledge of His will*, we fail to penetrate to the heart of the passage. Filled with *the knowledge of His will* concerning what? Concerning what your major in college should be? Who your spouse should be? Where you should buy a house? What stocks you should invest in? Whether to upgrade your I-phone? Order a Frappuccino or a cappuccino?

The end of verse 9 tells us what that will of God consists of: *all wisdom and spiritual understanding*. *Wisdom* is insight into what God has revealed.[43] *All* wisdom would be insight into the totality of God's revelation. *Spiritual understanding* is understanding that the Spirit gives. In other words, Paul is praying for believers to be filled with **what God has revealed to be spiritually important.**[44]

This insight is central to how we should pray for wisdom, and the importance of it cannot be overestimated. Note the expanding purpose in the text: to be filled with what God has revealed to be spiritually important **so that** we can walk *worthy of our Lord, fully pleasing Him* (v. 10).

A prayer for wisdom is not just a prayer for how I can better run my life so that things work out well for me. A prayer for wisdom is really a prayer to be filled with the knowledge of those things that are spiritually important so that I can conduct my life in a manner worthy of God.

What are those things that are spiritually important? Or, recast differently, what are those actions that please the Lord? Our passage in Colossians 1 lists four (which I have bolded in the text below):

> ... *that you may walk worthy of the Lord, fully pleasing Him,* **being fruitful in every good work** *and* **increasing in the knowledge of God; strengthened with all might,** *according to His glorious power, for all patience and longsuffering with joy;* **giving thanks to the Father** *who has qualified us to be partakers of the inheritance of the saints in the light (vv. 10-12).*

I summarize them this way:

(1) Producing every kind of good fruit in our lives

(2) Learning to know God better and better

(3) Being strong enough to patiently endure troubles with joy

(4) Gratefully acknowledging our unworthy inclusion in God's kingdom

These four make a great checklist of that which is spiritually important. They also have the potential to revolutionize the way you pray about your vacation, promotion, choice of college major, house to buy, or even your in-laws.

Rather than beg God for the "perfect" job or promotion so that you can live the American dream, why not pray (based on our fourfold checklist) something like this, "Lord, which job will make me more fruitful, guide me to know you better, strengthen me for trials, and make me grateful for Your salvation?" You will spend the majority of your waking hours at your work place—surely God has far more He wants to do through your career than just make you wealthy.

The same kind of praying could apply to almost any area of our lives. Is vacation merely an abandonment to American hedonism— entertaining yourself to the maximum your pocketbook will allow? Or is it possible that the Lord has some spiritual objective for your time together as a family? What if we were to approach marriage by praying this way: "Lord, you seem to be guiding my thoughts toward a certain young woman. Is this a relationship that will make me more fruitful, help me to know you better, strengthen me for trials, and make me grateful for Your salvation?" After all, God wants your marriage to teach you more about Him, not just make you happy. (Surely Hollywood's never-ending merry-go-round of divorce and remarriage demonstrates that pleasure-focused relationships are a dead-end street.)

One of the areas in which we pray too glibly for God's will relates to our health. We assume (typically) that God wants us well and healthy. Obviously, *we* want to be healthy, and God must surely feel the same way as we do. But what if your battle with cancer is what God wants to use in order to evangelize the local cancer ward? Or what if your heart problem is intended to slow you down and cause you to spend more time in prayer and Bible reading? What if your physical disorder that no specialist can diagnose accurately is intended to show onlookers how God strengthens a person to endure trials with joy? Or what if, as in Job's case, it is a kind of cosmic contest to see what it will take before you "curse God and die"?

Believe it or not, a miraculous cure may not always be what most glorifies God. Rather, it might be your stubborn rejoicing in Him and your growing longing for His kingdom that bring Him the most honor.

I am not saying it is wrong to pray for God to heal you. Or to want that. Personally, I am convinced that we sometimes do not experience deliverance from sickness because we do not take seriously enough James 5:14-16 and the frank confession of sin that divine healing (sometimes) demands.

On the other hand, we are wrong to somehow expect full healing to be the only real option worth praying about and to then grow bitter when God does not answer our prayers the way we want. J. I. Packer's words cut through our erroneous thinking:

> [W]e have recast Christianity into a mold that stresses happiness above holiness, blessings here above blessedness hereafter, health and wealth as God's best gifts, and death, especially early death, not as thankworthy deliverance from the miseries of a sinful world, but as the supreme disaster, and a constant challenge to faith in God's goodness. We have lost the New Testament's two-world perspective that views the next life as more important than this one.[45]

When my wife was battling her week-long migraine, her prayer was not just for healing but that she would be able to praise God in the midst of her pain. God not only granted eventual recovery, but also gave her some precious truths from the life of Job that she might never have gleaned if her week had been migraine-free. A missionary colleague of ours refers with gratefulness to his heart attack as the best thing that ever happened to him. It loosened him from his stranglehold on this life and taught him to love his Lord more than his ministry.

In summary, as we face decisions in our lives, we obviously need to pray. But how we pray is important. Spiritual priorities should govern our praying. In addition, we must commit ourselves unreservedly to obeying whatever wisdom the Lord gives us.

We also need to make sure that we do not confuse impressions with wisdom. We sometimes seek impressions (rather than wisdom) because we are lazy when it comes to decision-making. We want an answer written in the sky or penned by a finger on a wall.

…By doing so, however, we shortcut the process of what it often takes to become wise.

‹ 8 ›

Put Feet to Your Prayers for Wisdom

The plans of the diligent lead surely to plenty (Prov. 21:5)

Allow me to probe a little deeper into what you expect when you pray for wisdom. Let's say you are in a trial. You have come to the end of your logistical ability to handle it, and now you are at a loss. So you pray, like James 1 urges, for wisdom. When you pray for wisdom, what do you expect to happen? Should you look for a sign? Should you put out a fleece? Should you wait for some kind of unexpected peace? Timely advice in a Chinese fortune cookie? A lightning zap? A post on Facebook?

Have you ever considered the idea that a prayer for wisdom may be a prayer to which you need to "put feet"? God does not speak to us audibly today as He did in Bible times, nor do we have access to Urim and Thummim like David did, as we saw in the last chapter. This is not to say that God cannot communicate with us today. He can! But perhaps we fail to decode His answer because we do not understand the essence of what wisdom is or where to look for it.

Chokmah, the Old Testament word for wisdom, means "skill" or "ability." It is used for a number of skills—from waging war (Isa.

10:13) to crying at funerals (Jer. 9:16). The wisdom extolled in Proverbs is skill in fearing the Lord and in making choices that please Him. How does one acquire such skill? If we are seeking, for example, skill in rearing wise children, we do not just pray for it, turn on Monday night football, grab a bowl of popcorn, and wait for God to send us some. Wisdom ("skill") comes to those who cry out for it and then go searching.

> *My son, if you receive my words, and treasure my commands within you, so that you incline your ear to wisdom, and apply your heart to understanding; yes, if you cry out for discernment, and lift up your voice for understanding, if you seek her as silver, and search for her as for hidden treasures; then you will understand the fear of the LORD, and find the knowledge of God* (Prov. 2:1-5).

In other words—to refer back to our child-rearing example—we pray for God to give us wisdom, and then we "sweat through" the Bible passages on child rearing until their principles become engrained in us. The same can be said as we pursue skill in managing our finances, controlling our tongue, making friends, and developing a proper work ethic.

We almost automatically do this when it comes to making more mundane decisions. One year, for example, our Bible college was holding a pastor-training seminar in a mountainous area where a typhoon would shortly be blowing through. We prayed for wisdom as to whether we should cancel the seminar. What did we do then? We consulted various internet weather sites for more details about the typhoon: its expected velocity, arrival, departure, and pathway. We put feet to our prayer for direction by gathering more information about the approaching storm.

Similarly, we put feet to our prayers for wisdom by actively ransacking God's Word, meditating on its application, and then obeying. The very chapter in James that encourages us to pray for wisdom ends with this admonition:

*... **receive with meekness the implanted word**, which is able to save your souls. But **be doers of the word**, and not hearers only, deceiving yourselves. For if anyone is a hearer of the word and not a doer, he is like a man observing his natural face in a mirror; for he observes himself, goes away, and immediately forgets what kind of man he was. But he who looks into the perfect law of liberty and continues in it, and is not a forgetful hearer but a doer of the work, this one will be blessed in what he does* (vv. 21-25).

Some decisions may call for more than just a thorough search of Scripture. They may require what we often consider to be the more practical steps of doing research, seeking counsel, making observations, and weighing options. (Remember, a prayer for wisdom is a prayer that God will give you the information and discernment needed so that the wise choice becomes obvious.) Here is a basic plan of attack, which can be varied as necessary, for putting feet to your prayers for wisdom:

(1) Pray for wisdom.

This is the natural starting point, and it is what we devoted the last chapter to. James actually **commands** that we pray for wisdom.[46]

*If any of you lacks wisdom, **let him ask of God**, who gives to all liberally and without reproach, and it will be given to him* (1:5).

So, boldly pray for wisdom—whenever you find yourself in need of it—expect to receive it, and remain fully committed to obeying once it becomes clear what you should do. Then what? Put feet to your prayers for wisdom! Wisdom is the fruit of prayerful searching.

(2) Take the time to do research, gather data, and become knowledgeable.

Pray for wisdom and then start gathering data! Take the time and expend the energy to garner the knowledge necessary to make an informed decision or to plan wisely. Fact-finding may involve various forms of research: seeking counsel from people in the know, self-education, a magazine subscription, repeated trips to the library, web-based research, hands-on experience, or personal observation. Think of decision-making as getting a plane off the ground. The bigger the airplane, the bigger the runway needed. In the same way, the bigger the decision, the bigger the "runway" of knowledge needed.

Proverbs repeatedly extols the importance of knowledge:

*Also, it is not good for a soul to be **without knowledge**; and the hasty person makes mistakes with his feet* (19:2; my translation).

*Poor is he who works with a **negligent** [lazy] hand, but the hand of the **diligent** makes rich* (10:4; NASB).

*Every prudent man acts **with knowledge**, but a fool lays open his folly* (13:16).

*The simple believes every word, but the prudent **considers well** his steps* (14:15).

A few years ago, a small group from our ministry in the Philippines had the privilege to tour Israel. We were able to get slightly-discounted rates because we were traveling off-season in November and December. When I initially made the booking to join the tour, I did not realize the short duration of daylight at that time of year in Israel. The sun sets by around 4:30 pm, radically affecting how many sites we could visit in one day. I felt cheated when we had only forty-five minutes of sunlight remaining to see the huge archaeological dig at Beth-Shean. No wonder they discount tours in late November and early December!

A few years later, I was in charge of planning another trip to the Holy Land. You can be sure I took into consideration available sunlight, weather, and other criteria in planning the itinerary. Because I had more knowledge, I was able to make a better decision.

When my wife was expecting twin boys and the number of people in our family instantaneously jumped from six to eight, we knew we needed a larger vehicle than the mini-SUV we were driving at the time. I started doing research into the various van options in the Philippines. We wanted a diesel because diesel fuel was cheaper and widely available. I also wanted an automatic, if possible, since my wife does not drive a standard transmission. As I investigated further, I learned some pertinent information. A number of the available van options were actually imports from Japan or Singapore and had been converted from right-hand drive to left-hand drive. These vans often have unusual or recurring problems because of the conversion process. My research convinced me to avoid these models. Eventually I settled on a van that ran on diesel fuel, sported an automatic transmission, and had not been converted; it has served us well. However, it required talking to people, visiting used car lots, test-driving various models, and asking the right questions.

Several years ago, I heard of a church whose pulpit committee narrowly averted a fiasco. The pulpit committee considered or interviewed numerous candidates. Several had respectable resumes and likable personalities. One man in particular interested them, and they were on the verge of starting the official process of calling him to candidate when, almost by chance, they happened upon newspaper articles that reported on some of his previous acts of extremely bizarre behavior. It was a wake-up call to the pulpit committee. God had delivered them from a serious mistake. (He had answered their prayer for wisdom in leading them across those newspaper articles.) They realized that they needed to do their homework thoroughly on any future candidate.

All of these stories serve to reinforce the necessity of taking time to do research, gather data, and become knowledgeable. This is part of the skill you pray for when you ask God for wisdom. It reminds us again of our theme verse for this chapter:

*The plans of the diligent will surely bring profit, while the **hasty** will surely experience poverty* (Prov. 21:5; my translation).

Part of not being *hasty* is taking the time to talk to the right people, ask the right questions, and gather data from the right resources. It pays off in the long run.

God can do special things. I definitely do not want to put God in a box of my finite dimensions. However, if the Bible extols the value of knowledge, would you not agree that God intends us to gather knowledge as a part of making wise decisions? On a number of occasions, I have impulse-purchased or acted on a sudden impression. Some of those decisions turned out well. Others I regretted. I have generally found I make better decisions when I build a runway of knowledge of the appropriate length.

(3) Consider carefully what Scripture says about your decision.

In a previous chapter, we proposed a fivefold grid for shining the light of Scripture on our pathway:

- ‣ Clear (and relevant) commands

- ‣ Passages that specifically address situations (decisions) like yours

- ‣ Biblical characters (good and bad) in life circumstances comparable to yours

- ‣ General principles that should influence your actions

- ‣ What God is teaching you in your regular personal time with Him

As we put feet to our prayers for wisdom and begin to research and gather data, a major part of that process must include thinking through what Scripture says about our decision.

I have personally found it helpful to make two columns on a sheet of paper or in a computer spreadsheet. In one column, I list biblical principles in support of a decision; in the other, those "against" it. I can then compare the scriptural evidence and assess where the strongest biblical support lies.

Another approach is to take five sheets of paper and label each of them at the top with one of the five categories of passages listed above. You can shorthand it this way: commands, relevant passages, biblical characters, general principles, and personal devotions. Then, think through each category and write down passages that deserve inclusion or further study. If your knowledge of the Bible is still rather meager, you may want to use some kind of a topical Scripture guide or a Thompson Chain Reference Bible to locate relevant passages. A number of websites also offer an easy means of doing word or topical searches. For example, www.blueletterbible.org (also available as an app) allows you to search for almost any word or verse in your choice of over a dozen English Bible versions. Or ask a more knowledgeable Christian to recommend any passages that they think would have bearing on your situation.

This is such an important step in planning diligently that I think it is worth the space to work through a hypothetical example together.

Let's postulate a newly-married couple without any children. The man has just been offered his dream job in northern Montana. It will afford them the opportunity to buy land, do some farming on the side, and hunt on their own property. His wife is particularly excited about it since she loves horses and sees this as a chance to have the horse ranch she always wanted. As he continues his research into the job offer and flies out for a second interview, he begins to realize that there is no good church in the area. In fact, the closest Bible-preaching church is over one hour away. Getting there regularly and faithfully will be a real challenge. Also, his prospective employer reveals that he will be expected to work regularly on Sundays, further complicating the ease of making it to church regularly. He is confronted in himself with this question, "Should I take a job where I will have little or no church involvement and spiritual fellowship?"

He pulls out his Bible, goes to his favorite Bible research website, and gets out five pieces of paper at the top of which he writes the five categories we have cited above. He then begins to work through each category:

Commands: One clear command he thinks of is the Great Commission (Matt. 28:19-20). How can he possibly fulfill his responsibility to make disciples if he has no church where he can bring people to be taught and to be baptized? He then recalls Hebrews 10:25, *not forsaking the assembling of ourselves together, as is the manner of some, but exhorting one another, and so much the more as you see the Day approaching.* Clearly, God wants believers to gather regularly for mutual spiritual encouragement.

Relevant passages: As he studies about the body of Christ, he comes across 1 Corinthians 12 and is reminded that God has gifted him with spiritual gifts so that they can be **used**, which will be almost impossible if he pursues the job offer before him.

Biblical characters: The first biblical character to come to his mind was Lot, Abraham's nephew. He thought about how Lot sacrificed the spiritual good of his family because of the place he chose to live (Gen. 13:10-13; 19:14ff). He wonders if Lot's life (and the disaster that ensued) might contain a warning to him. As he meditates further, he is struck by some of the parallels between his situation and Lot's: moving his family … provision too good to be true … questionable spiritual influence.

General principles: He reflects on his duty to any children the Lord might give him and his wife to rear them in the *training and admonition of the Lord* (Eph. 6:4). Other passages like Deuteronomy 6:7 further speak of this responsibility:

You shall teach them [God's Words] diligently to your children, and shall talk of them when you sit in your house, when you walk by the way, when you lie down, and when you rise up.

He realizes that the passage does not mention the church specifically. In fact, it puts the ball in his court (not the church's) to disciple his children, but without any spiritual leadership or fellowship, he doubts he can do the job well.

Personal devotions: The particular morning he bows his head and asks God unreservedly for wisdom is the same morning that he reads Psalm 42, where the Psalmist is literally longing for the opportunity to once again worship God corporately at the Temple (since some unmentioned circumstance is preventing it for the time being). The passage makes him think about the priority of worship for a believer. If godly men in the past have so highly valued corporate worship, should he put himself in a place where he knows he will have limited or no access to it?

For the young man in our example above, his pathway became increasingly clear. Growing knowledge about the situation (research) had led him to an understanding of the spiritual famine he would face in his new location, and the second interview—he was not just hastily accepting the job—brought out an additional very important piece of information (he would be assigned to the Sunday shift). Through this, he was able to pinpoint the spiritual question that needed to be answered, and then work through what Scripture said in order to answer that question.

(4) Prayerfully lay all your research and all your Scripture passages before the Lord.

What do you do when you have researched the facts and ransacked the Scriptures? The following verses give an answer:

Commit your way to the LORD, trust also in Him, and He shall bring it to pass (Psa. 37:5).

In all your ways acknowledge Him, and He shall direct your paths (Prov. 3:6).

Commit your works to the LORD, and your thoughts will be established (Prov. 16:3).

I would summarize it this way: lay before the Lord what you have learned. Bring before Him the pros and cons. Talk through with Him the research you have done. Weigh before Him the Scriptural principles that apply. Expect the Holy Spirit to illumine your pathway.

Do not hurry this step. You may need to set aside a Saturday morning or a weekday evening. If you are married, include your wife in your deliberations, get her input, and then together commit your works to the Lord in prayer.

(5) Make plans (decisions) on the basis of what you have found, knowing that God is directing your steps.

My experience is that when I have honestly worked through the steps above, I do not typically end up in a "multiple choice" situation, where every option is just as good as the other. Call it the Lord giving His promised wisdom. Call it illumination. Call it the Holy Spirit speaking through the living Word of God. Call it the Lord "establishing" my thoughts or placing something on my heart (Neh. 7:5). I am not exactly sure what to call it, but often by this step a certain course of action commends itself to me above all others.

"PRAYER AND PAINS"[47]

What I am essentially arguing for in this chapter is the use of means to acquire wisdom in our decision-making. Not means divorced from prayer (or the Spirit), but means bathed with prayer in the Spirit! Too often, we view research, data-collecting, talking with experts, and surveying the options available as almost unspiritual. A spiritual person, the reasoning goes, does not need to do all that work—he can just pray and God will communicate to his spirit a clear "yes" or "no" answer.

In actuality, a genuinely spiritual person will cry out in total dependence upon God for wisdom and then use all of the resources at his or her disposal in order to search out that wisdom. He (or she) moves forward with the confidence that the God to whom he has directed his prayers will oversee every step of his research, every piece of information he uncovers, every advisor he consults, and every verse of Scripture he ponders. Diligence in planning, done in complete dependence upon God, is how we put feet to our prayers for wisdom.

Take one parting look at our chapter's theme verse:

The plans of the diligent will surely bring profit, while the hasty will surely experience poverty (Prov. 21:5; my translation).

... Be ready, however, for possible adjustments to all your best-laid plans.

◄ **9** ►

Anticipate Possible Redirection

A man's heart plans his way, but the LORD directs his steps (Prov. 16:9)

Early in his ministry in China, J. Hudson Taylor was evangelizing a place called Swatow with a likeminded Scottish missionary by the name of William Burns. Opposition to their work was real, and they needed a clear breakthrough for the gospel. In early July, the chief mandarin of that area became very ill, and native doctors failed to help him. Taylor successfully treated him, and as a result, a door for ongoing ministry swung wide open. The much-prayed-for breakthrough had come. They began to lay plans for a clinic in Swatow as a headquarters for preaching the gospel.

Taylor, however, needed the medical supplies that he had left in Shanghai. Providentially, as it must have seemed at the time, he was granted free passage on a ship heading to Shanghai. Everything seemed to be favoring their preparations. Taylor had no idea of how God would re-order the plans that he had made with William Burns.

The last couple of chapters may have made it sound like the pursuit of God's will is easy and automated. Offer up a prayer, do a little research, come up with a few Bible passages, lay out a plan, and go your merry way.

Not so fast! Sometimes the Spirit of God changes our plans.

On one of my trips to Israel, we had a Jewish guide who quipped, "You want to know how to make God laugh? Make a plan." The aphorism "Man proposes, but God disposes" is at least as old as Thomas à Kempis.[48]

Numerous verses in Scripture assert something similar:

The preparations of the heart belong to man, but the answer of the tongue is from the LORD (Prov. 16:1).

Commit your works to the LORD, and your thoughts will be established (Prov. 16:3).

A man's heart plans his way, but the LORD directs his steps (Prov. 16:9).

A man's steps are of the LORD; how then can a man understand his own way (Prov. 20:24)?

All of these verses juxtapose human planning with divine sovereignty. At the same time, God's sovereignty regularly trumps human planning. We make plans based on God's Word and thoughtful research, submit them to the Lord, proceed to work them, and then watch Him—on occasion—re-direct those very plans. *The best-laid plans of godly men sometimes take a bend!*

Someone might ask, "Why then should I plan if God is going to redirect my steps anyway?" Consider the following reasons:

> ⯈ Almost without trying, humans lay plans (Prov. 16:1). It is probably accurate to conclude that it is impossible for us *not* to do so.

> ⯈ Certain Scripture passages encourage careful planning (Prov. 14:15; 21:5). We are to pursue the pathway of wisdom, and this requires all-out effort.

- ▷ Planning reveals the desires of our hearts. It shows where our treasures are, like when David vocalized his desire to build a Temple for the Lord (2 Sam. 7:2).

- ▷ It is easier to steer a moving car than a parked one. God directs us as we step out in faith and do what we *believe* to be His will for us in a given situation.

- ▷ God's redirection is not normally radical. When we follow His guidelines for decision-making, we will generally find ourselves on the right pathway with only "minor" adjustments necessary. Picture it like someone steering a car along a major interstate. Occasional nudges of the steering wheel are all it generally takes to keep the car in between the white (or yellow) lines.

My favorite passage on divine redirection comes from the life of Paul, where on one occasion during his second missionary journey the Holy Spirit rerouted him twice (Acts 16:6-10).

> *And they went through the region of Phrygia and Galatia, having been* **forbidden by the Holy Spirit** *to speak the word in Asia. And when they had come up to Mysia, they attempted to go into Bithynia, but* **the Spirit of Jesus did not allow them**. *So, passing by Mysia, they went down to Troas. And a vision appeared to Paul in the night: a man of Macedonia was standing there, urging him and saying, "Come over to Macedonia and help us." And when Paul had seen the vision, immediately we sought to go on into Macedonia, concluding that God had called us to preach the gospel to them* (ESV).

In order to understand the passage, we have to understand the sequence of events:

- ▷ Paul attempts to enter Asia, but the Holy Spirit forbids him (v. 6).

- ▷ He preaches the gospel in Phrygia and Galatia instead.

- ▷ He then heads to Mysia (v. 7).

121

- From there he attempts to enter Bithynia but the Holy Spirit stops him (v. 7).

- He opts instead for Troas, a coastal city of the Aegean Sea (v. 8).

- There he receives the "Macedonian vision" (v. 9).

- He concludes that God's "open door" lies across the Aegean Sea (v. 10).

Why did the Holy Spirit twice redirect Paul from his chosen course of travel? It becomes clear when the Lord opens up a large door of opportunity that he was not anticipating. This passage illustrates how divine redirection works and provides a number of helpful principles in the process. Consider the following:

(1) Even godly people do not always know exactly what God wants them to do.

We all recognize the Apostle Paul to be one of the early church's greatest missionaries and one of the godliest men in the New Testament. He, in fact, is the one man above any other (except Christ) that we are commanded to *follow* or *imitate* (1 Cor. 4:16; 11:1; Phil. 3:17; 4:9; 1 Thess. 1:6; 2 Thess. 3:9).

Paul, however, attempted twice to go places God did not want him to go. Is Paul in rebellion? Unlikely! Rather, Paul did not know exactly where God wanted him to go. Centuries earlier, Abraham also "went out, not knowing whither he went" (Heb. 11:8). The point? Godly people, in spite of their sincere pursuit of God's will, may still sometimes come short of explicit assurance of the direction they should take.

The name Amy Carmichael is synonymous with Dohnavur, India, but she actually began her missionary career as a candidate with the China Inland Mission. Her health forced her to abandon any plans for China, and she left the CIM for the Church Missionary Society. Her first foreign missionary endeavor was in Japan, where after only fifteen months poor health compelled her to return home to Britain. Her next venture in Ceylon did not work out either.

Hearing that the climate in Bangalore, India, would suit her health, Amy went (under yet another mission board) and never left. There in India—Dohnavur, to be specific—she found her life's calling and started a work that continues to this day. Almost from the beginning, Amy knew God wanted her in missions in Asia, but she did not know exactly where.

Chances are that few of you are doing today what you thought you would be doing five years ago. We plan, but God often reorders our steps. When my wife and I married, our plan was to spend one year in the States before returning to Asia as missionaries. Instead, we spent four years in a ministry in Wisconsin before God sent us back to Asia. We had the right idea, but the wrong timetable.

If you know that God may change your plans—someone might ask—shouldn't you put everything on hold until everything is crystal clear and you are 100% confident of every detail? Not if you follow Paul's example. Our passage in Acts 16 shows Paul pushing forward with his plans.

(2) Work your plans based on what you believe you should do.

Paul was not stubbornly rebelling against the Lord when he attempted to enter Asia and Bithynia (Acts 16:6-7); he was simply working his plan. He knew his calling was to the Gentiles who had never heard (Rom. 15:20). Asia fit that bill, and so did Bithynia. (Interestingly, Paul ended up in Asia for three years on his next missionary journey, and Peter writes to believers in Bithynia. In God's timing, a work was started in those regions.) As Paul worked his plans, God used those very travels to steer him where He wanted him. Paul had the right idea but the wrong place, or at least the wrong timetable.

We see a somewhat similar situation in the life of David. David expresses to Nathan the prophet his desire to build a Temple for the Lord (2 Sam. 7:2). Nathan's initial response is one of encouragement:

Then Nathan said to the king, "Go, do all that is in your heart, for the LORD is with you" (v. 3).

Nathan's words are good advice for believers with a heart completely devoted to the Lord: *Go, do what is in your heart to do for the Lord!* Make a plan, and then work your plan.

Few people have ever heard of Robert Morrison, the father of Protestant missions to China. Robert Morrison was converted at age fifteen and by age seventeen was already contemplating missions. His sickly mother, however, pressed him for a promise that he would not go into missions until she died. When his mother died during his twentieth year, he was free to pursue his burden for missions. He entered a missionary training program, not knowing exactly where God wanted him, but with the prayer "that God would station him in that part of the missionary field where the difficulties were greatest and to all human appearances the most insurmountable." As Morrison worked his plan for missions, God eventually steered him toward China, where he spent the remainder of his short fifty-two years in exhausting pioneer labors.

(3) Allow, even expect, the Spirit of God to redirect or re-shape your plan.

Twice, the Holy Spirit redirected Paul. The passage does not say exactly how the Holy Spirit communicated to him. We do not know if there was some kind of audible voice, or if a circumstantial door closed. What it does say is that *they were forbidden by the Holy Spirit* and *the Spirit did not permit them* (Acts 16:6-7).

If we take what happened to Paul as a kind of paradigm for Christians in general, we can assume that the Spirit of God will similarly sometimes redirect or re-shape our plans. He has many ways of redirecting us—through Scripture, counselors, circumstances, a change in our desires, unanticipated tragedies, and a variety of other means. As we work our plans, we must be sensitive to His potential redirection.

David, like Paul, also experienced a closed door. The same prophet who told David, *Go, do all that is in your heart, for the LORD is with you*, had to come back and inform him of God's "red light." Incidentally, the redirection for David was almost immediate—*that night* (2 Sam. 7:4). God works with us similarly. His redirection is always perfectly timed and coincides exactly with His plan, if not always with ours.

Perhaps our greatest challenge is allowing the Lord to redirect us. Too often, when God closes a door, we stand there and jiggle the door knob. Our heart is set on our own course of action. We have fallen in love with our plans and cannot part with them.

George Müller described his first step in finding God's will this way, "I seek at the beginning to get my heart into such a state that it has no will of its own in regard to a given matter. Nine-tenths of the trouble with people generally is just here. Nine-tenths of the difficulties are overcome when our hearts are ready to do the Lord's will, whatever it may be."

This challenge of submitting our hearts may be why the Bible emphasizes committing our ways to the Lord (Psa. 37:5; Prov. 3:5-6; 16:3). Don't hold on to your best-laid plans; hold on to your God. Trust Him to be your Pilot through the storm-tossed sea of life.

If we will submit to the Lord's redirection, down the road we will eventually realize how foolish our initial resistance was. Did we really think that we knew better than a good, sovereign, and omniscient God?

Armored cars in Manila have unusually small windows (because of the very real threat of armed robbery)—so tiny, in fact, that I sometimes wonder how the driver can possibly see the buses, tricycles, jeepneys, pedicabs, cars, bicycles, pedestrians, and stray dogs milling around him. He has a very limited view of the road in front of him. Contrast that with a helicopter pilot hovering several hundred feet above the roadway; he has a far better view! We are, in some ways, like that armored car driver. In spite of our best-laid plans, we frankly have a very limited view of what lies ahead or around us. God, however, sees our whole pathway from beginning to end. Can't we trust Him when He shuts a door and opens a different one?

God's reordering of our steps ought actually to minister to us the assurance that a believer in genuine pursuit of God's plan for his or her life will find it very difficult to wander indefinitely outside of it.

Though he fall, he shall not be utterly cast down; For the LORD upholds him with His hand (Psa. 37:24).

(4) Look for the "new" open door.

God closes certain doors in order to open others. He does not close doors to disappoint us, but to protect us; not to pester us, but to better place us. One of my former missionary colleagues would regularly exclaim, "God is a good manager!" His point was that God knows best how to strategically assign His soldiers. Paul experienced this. God shut the door to Asia and Bithynia because He was opening Macedonia. God was calling Paul to take the gospel across the Aegean Sea to modern-day Europe, and He had people there in whose hearts He was already working (Acts 16:14, 31-34).

Think again of our example of David. David expressed his desire to build a Temple for the Lord, and God said no. Is that the end of the road for David? No! Actually, it was just the beginning. God turned the tables on him and revealed that rather than his building a house for God, God was building a "house" for him: God established David's line as a dynasty through which would come the long-awaited Messiah. God opened a door that David could never have envisioned. The weight of what God had revealed to David—this newly-opened door—led David to exclaim, *Who am I, O Lord GOD? And what is my house, that You have brought me this far* (2 Sam. 7:18)? David was overwhelmed with God's plan. It was far better than his.

To be honest, David was not entirely off-base to desire to build a Temple for the Lord. He had the right idea. God would, in fact, use David's son Solomon to build the Temple. Many of the resources that Solomon used to build the Temple were actually prepared and amassed by his father David (1 Chron. 22:6-17). Most of the organization of the Temple Levites, singers, and priests came from David (chs. 23-26). The design for the Temple came from David, revealed to him by God (28:11-19). David did have a part in building the Temple, just not in the way that he thought. God had something greater He was doing. It goes back to that helicopter view we alluded to earlier.

BACK TO SWATOW

Remember Hudson Taylor, blissfully boating off to Shanghai to fulfill the plans he and William Burns had prayerfully made? Unfortunately, when he arrived in Shanghai, he found that a fire had destroyed all his cached medical supplies. His only recourse was to make the three- or four-day trip to Ningpo to Dr. Parker, a medical missionary friend of his, in order to get more supplies. As he traveled there, he was robbed and left penniless. Consequently, he did not arrive in Ningpo until August. Dr. Parker gave him supplies, and at the end of the month he was ready to leave.

He then encountered another delay: some missionaries needed his help to escort them to Shanghai; he must wait until they were ready to leave Ningpo. In the end, Taylor did not return to Shanghai until October. Three precious months had been wasted! He placed his supplies on board a ship for Swatow. Then he received the bad news: William Burns had been arrested and evicted from Swatow. All plans were off! The door had closed. The two men, in fact, would never see each other again.

A tragedy? In some ways. A new open door? Unbelievably so! All the difficulties and delays were merely God's way of redirecting Taylor's steps into his life's work, which was initially based at Ningpo, and to his future wife, Maria Dyer. God, as Taylor later learned to say, is the Great Circumstance. God was the One who had created, saved, called, and equipped Taylor and was simply placing his chosen servant in the most strategic location to fulfill *His* purposes.

‹ **10** ›

Assess Your Open Doors

My son, if sinners entice you, do not consent (Prov. 1:10)

My wife and I were chatting with a couple sitting near us before a Sunday afternoon lecture. It was the winter of 2003. (Virtually any time of year is winter in Wisconsin, where we were at the time.)

The conversation shifted to their daughter who, with her family, was coming home from their missionary work in Cambodia for a furlough. Another missionary, the couple pointed out, had left the field permanently, leaving behind only one remaining missionary family to oversee all the various ministries.

"You," they suddenly decided (pointing at us), "should spend your summer vacation helping the Johnsons" (the overtaxed missionary couple still in Cambodia).

A door that we had never before given any consideration to had just opened. Was this the voice of God? Or a distraction? How could we know the difference?

OPEN DOORS CAN BE GOOD OR BAD

Too many people operate on the principle that an open door in their life must be God's will. If it weren't, then why would God allow it to happen? However, we just saw from the life of Hudson Taylor that not every open door is one that God wants us to go through. Swatow, for example, wasn't; Ningpo was.

Think of an open door as an invitation or opportunity that can be either good or bad. In and of itself, an opportunity may look quite innocent and even attractive: an acceptance letter with an attached scholarship guarantee from the college of your choice, an email from a relative asking you to spend the summer working with him on his farm, or an advertisement to buy what you have always wanted at zero money down and zero interest for twelve months.

What we should immediately recognize, though, is that not all opportunities are as innocent as they may first appear. In Scripture, danger lurked behind some open doors:

> ▷ Satan's invitation to Eve to eat the forbidden fruit.
>
> *Then the serpent said to the woman, "You will not surely die. For God knows that in the day you eat of it your eyes will be opened, and you will be like God, knowing good and evil"* (Gen. 3:4-5).

> ▷ The King of Sodom's generous invitation to Abram to help himself to all the booty seized in battle.
>
> *Now the king of Sodom said to Abram, "Give me the persons, and take the goods for yourself"* (14:21).

> ▷ Balak's invitation to Balaam to curse the people of God and receive a handsome reward.
>
> *And they came to Balaam and said to him, "Thus says Balak the son of Zippor: 'Please let nothing hinder you from coming to me; for I will*

certainly honor you greatly, and I will do whatever you say to me. Therefore please come, curse this people for me'" (Num. 22:16-17).

On other occasions, biblical characters viewed an opportunity as divinely given and went through it with God's apparent blessing:

> Crown-prince Jonathan set up a game plan by which he would know whether he and his armor bearer should singlehandedly attack the Philistines. When the Philistine garrison invited him to ascend into their midst, he took that as a divinely given opportunity.

> *Then Jonathan said, "Very well, let us cross over to these men, and we will show ourselves to them. If they say thus to us, 'Wait until we come to you,' then we will stand still in our place and not go up to them. But if they say thus, 'Come up to us,' then we will go up. For the LORD has delivered them into our hand, and this will be a sign to us."*

> *So both of them showed themselves to the garrison of the Philistines. And the Philistines said, "Look, the Hebrews are coming out of the holes where they have hidden." Then the men of the garrison called to Jonathan and his armorbearer, and said, "Come up to us, and we will show you something." Jonathan said to his armorbearer, "Come up after me, for the LORD has delivered them into the hand of Israel"* (1 Sam. 14:8-12).

> Peter accepted the invitation to evangelize the Roman centurion Cornelius and went.

> *And they said, "Cornelius the centurion, a just man, one who fears God and has a good reputation among all the nation of the Jews, was divinely instructed by a holy angel to summon you to his house, and to hear words from you." Then he invited them in and lodged them. On the next day Peter went away with them, and some brethren from Joppa accompanied him* (Acts 10:22-23).

> ⯈ As we saw in the last chapter, Paul regarded the Macedonian vision as God's clear redirection to those living on the western side of the Aegean Sea.

> *And a vision appeared to Paul in the night. A man of Macedonia stood and pleaded with him, saying, "Come over to Macedonia and help us." Now after he had seen the vision, immediately we sought to go to Macedonia, concluding that the Lord had called us to preach the gospel to them* (Acts 16:9-10).

The above examples prove the point that open doors can be either good or bad. To assume that every open door in our life is one that we should pursue is about as prudent as closing our eyes, opening any physical door we come to, and bounding in impetuously. As the saying goes, "Some open doors lead to empty elevator shafts."

Far worse even than falling into an empty elevator shaft is walking through spiritually harmful open doors. We need to evaluate the open doors that come our way, and Proverbs 1:10-19 provides some very practical advice for doing so.[49]

> **My son,** *if sinners entice you, do not consent. If they say, "Come with us, let us lie in wait to shed blood; let us lurk secretly for the innocent without cause; let us swallow them alive like Sheol, and whole, like those who go down to the Pit; we shall find all kinds of precious possessions, we shall fill our houses with spoil; cast in your lot among us, let us all have one purse . . ."*

> **My son,** *do not walk in the way with them, keep your foot from their path; for their feet run to evil, and they make haste to shed blood. Surely, in vain the net is spread in the sight of any bird; but they lie in wait for their own blood, They lurk secretly for their own lives. So are the ways of everyone who is greedy for gain; it takes away the life of its owners.*

If you look through the verses above, you will see the expression *my son* used twice (vv. 10, 15). These two occurrences of *my son* introduce two fatherly warnings about invitations. The father's warnings not only

132

provide needed advice for his son but also give guidance to those of us listening in as to how we can assess the invitations or open doors in our lives.

WHEN TO REFUSE CERTAIN INVITATIONS

The first five verses (vv. 10-14) contain two *if* clauses in which the father is warning his son **when** to refuse certain invitations.

When ("if") the invitation comes from a *sinner*—one on a decided pathway of wrongdoing—then one should refuse it (v. 10).

When ("if") the invitation is to wound and destroy the innocent—arguably, somebody who is righteous—the invitation should, once again, be refused (vv. 11-14). After all, such a goal is incompatible with God's revealed will and is fueled by the unbiblical motive of greed (vv. 13-14).

WHY TO REFUSE CERTAIN INVITATIONS

The father's second warning to his son explains **why** to refuse certain invitations (vv. 15-19). Those plotting the destruction of others in order to fill their own pockets are self-deceived as to whose destruction they are hurrying toward (v. 16). They are actually lying in wait for their own blood (v. 18).

They are sillier (stupider) than a hunted animal (vv. 17-19). An animal is wiser than to fall into a trap he sees being made, but these sinners actually make their own trap. They teach us a lesson about greed we should never forget: you may take your cut, but you will lose your soul in the process.

From these two fatherly warnings about when and why to refuse invitations, I have formulated four questions to use in assessing the open doors in our lives:

(1) What is the spiritual condition of the person inviting you?

The father opened his advice to his son with these words, "*If **sinners** entice you . . .*" (my emphasis). The character of the person extending the invitation is important.

Who, for example, is the person inviting you to attend a different church? Who is the person suggesting you move to their apartment or start working at their place of employment? Do their Facebook pictures reveal that they are the type of person with whom you should become an intimate friend? (Their likes and dislikes indicate the direction of their life.)

An unsaved friend or family member may be wise in a number of areas, but their perspective will typically be more materialistic in its orientation. They will not readily understand, for example, that a believer should not prioritize making money if it comes at the expense of neglecting biblical priorities.

By the way, the inviter does not always have to be a person. It could be your own flesh, the unredeemable part of you that constantly beckons you to satisfy its desires. That inner invitation to go back to a seamy website or to waste time instead of studying is the voice of your flesh. Do you really want to obey it again and give it that much more of a hold over your actions?

Another potential source of enticement is one's cultural way of doing things. When Sarai, for example, offered Abram her maidservant, Hagar, in order to acquire an heir, she was acting in a way that was quite appropriate to her culture. She was the one who was barren and unable to produce a child, and she was therefore responsible to obtain for her husband the heir he deserved. In Sarah's world, any progeny of Abram and Hagar's would be considered hers, since Hagar was her servant. Sarah's invitation to Abram to take Hagar was a cultural norm, but it was not what God wanted. Before you blindly mimic what everybody else is doing around you, ask yourself, "Is this rooted in sinful or unwholesome aspects of my culture?"

(2) What are your real goals/motives for pursuing the open door?

In Proverbs 1:11-14, the father spells out for his son the content of the sinners' invitation: to kill innocent people in order to steal from them and enrich themselves. Their invitation is expressly unbiblical, both as to the goals pursued and the motive enjoined.

When confronted with an open door, honestly ask yourself, "What is my true goal?" Then probe further: "What does God's Word say about my goal?" (Keep in mind that sometimes our *stated* goal differs from our *real* goal.) For example, what is your true goal in wanting to get married? To find emotional security? Or to live out God's purposes for marriage? What is your underlying goal for choosing to study medicine? Is it because it offers the highest potential salary? Or because it exactly fits who God made you to be?

In addition, we must be painfully candid about our motives. As Samuel the judge aged and his sons proved corrupt, the children of Israel began to ask for a king. In a sense, their stated desire was not wrong. Having a king was, in fact, something God had planned for them. What was wrong, however, was their motive—*to be like the other nations* (1 Sam. 8:5, 20).

Lot moved to Sodom because he noticed the fertility of the surrounding area (Gen. 13:10). Did his decision reflect a veiled motive of covetousness? Or an honest desire to adequately provide for his family?

As you assess life's open doors, ask the hard "why" questions. Be brutal with yourself.

Why is she the "girl of your dreams"?

Your primary motive might be visual appeal, not a sense that God made her to help you accomplish your life's mission.

Why do you want to marry a certain man?

My wife and I counseled a young lady who had married a man because she thought he would be successful in life, not because she wanted to help him accomplish his deepest aspirations. No wonder she was ready to bail out of the marriage when life with him did not achieve her financial ideals.

Why are you working long overtime hours?

The *stated* goal might be to provide for your family, but maybe your *real* motive is to escape pressures at home (an unlovable wife, a less-than-respectable husband, or challenging children).

Sometimes we jump through open doors to escape the harsh realities of our God-given circumstances, only to land in a worse situation. Christ may want you, with His help, to weather the storms in your life, not abandon ship!

(3) Have you adequately considered the consequences?

In our Proverbs passage, the father warns the son of the consequences if he accepts the invitation to kill and steal (vv. 15-19). His advice draws attention to the importance of thinking through the consequences of a given course of action.

Lot (to pick on him again) based his decision on the lushness of the land near Sodom. His goal was perhaps noble: to better provide for his family … to work a little less… to discontinue nomadic tent life. From a human standpoint, his choice was a good one: he had much cattle and needed a place with abundant green grass.

He did not, however, carefully think through the consequences of his decision. When Lot pitched his tent near Sodom, he did so in an area renowned for its wickedness.

But the men of Sodom were exceedingly wicked and sinful against the LORD (Gen. 13:13).

Sodom's grass fed his cattle, but its morals ate up his children.

(4) Are your spiritual "fathers" forbidding you?

Twice, the father urges his son against accepting the sinners' invitation. What are *your* spiritual fathers saying about the open door confronting you? Have you even asked them? Some people run from the advice of spiritually-wise people because they fear the answer will contradict their own plans. However, fleeing from godly advice is fraught with peril. The father is not forbidding his son to join in with sinners because he hates his son. Rather, he has detected that his son is still a bit naïve and potentially open to the persuasions of unprincipled people. He does not want his son to start down a course of action that will eventually ruin him. Similarly, God does not put "spiritual fathers" in our lives in order to take away all our fun. They can often see our circumstances more clearly than we can. They have seen enough human shipwrecks to know when others are drifting toward the same dangerous shoals.

TEMPTATION OR TEST?

Someone may ask, "If I am not supposed to take advantage of an open door in my life, then why is it there? Shouldn't I view it as providential?"

Some open doors are actually temptations. Not every party is one you should attend. Not everything you see advertised is something you should buy, even if it is on sale. Not every friend is one you should move in with, even if you will be saving money on rent and utilities (and able to put more in the offering every Sunday—oh, how spiritual sounding our reasoning can be).

Actually, an open door could be either a temptation or a test.

A temptation is an open door to do wrong, masterfully crafted by Satan as a wonderful opportunity.

Seldom are Satan's invitations as clearly unbiblical as what we find in Proverbs 1:10-19. Satan is a master of deceit. He speaks with a hiss not a shout; he masquerades as an angel of light. Your situation will often be more like Abraham's, where only the eye of faith could help him see the devastating consequences if he accepted the King of Sodom's handsome offer (Gen. 14:21).[50]

Satan may use people as His instruments. That's why the character of the person suggesting a certain course of action is so important. Nehemiah fortunately recognized Shemaiah's suggestion to hide in the Temple as a Satanic snare. To save his life by hiding in the Temple, an action forbidden to anyone who was not a priest, would have permanently damaged his reputation and effectively halted the work on Jerusalem's walls (Neh. 6:10-13).

The charred remains (sometimes literally) of those who fell into the cunningly devised temptations that Satan masked as wonderful opportunities litter the ash heap of history. Cain, Balaam, Korah, Achan, Ahab, Judas Iscariot, and Demas all bit Satan's bait and tasted of its awful consequences.

A test is an open door God might use to expose how sinful you really are.

King Hezekiah was a God-fearing man who trusted the Lord during some unusually difficult circumstances. Pride, however, clung to his heart, and reared its ugly head when emissaries from Babylon showed up, ready to be impressed by the miracle-stories of deliverance they had heard about. Hezekiah saw the Babylonian emissaries as an opportunity to show off his kingdom. From God's vantage point, their coming was a test during which He *left Hezekiah, to try him, that he might know all that was in his heart* (2 Chron. 32:31). God may allow some open doors as a way of exposing who we really are and bringing us to a sharpened dependence upon Him for spiritual victory.

CAMBODIA OR NOT?

As my wife and I prayed about the open door to minister in Cambodia, we had to think through the very questions we just worked through above. The right people were behind the invitation. In fact, our pastor (our "spiritual father") fully supported the idea. Our motives were right—to assist a missionary for the gospel's sake—and it fit what we believed to be the direction of our future ministry—to live and work in Asia.

The consequences were perhaps the toughest to face. At the time, SARS was making its deadly march across Asia. Our infant daughter was too young to receive the recommended injections for travelers to Cambodia. My wife, we discovered, was pregnant with our second child. We would be staying with missionaries we hardly knew in a country that we did not know but was reputed to be physically and spiritually challenging. We knew, however, that difficulties do not automatically negate the validity of an open door (1 Cor. 16:8-9). Going, we eventually decided, was a matter of obedience to God's will for us, and we would trust God for the consequences of obedience.

We did face a number of challenges during that summer of ministry—including debilitating bouts with Dengue Fever—and God delivered us from every one of them. The comfort while we were in the midst of those challenges was knowing that our summer was an open door that we had biblically assessed and ascertained to be in the path of duty.

◄ 11 ►

Advice for Seeking Advice

The way of a fool is right in his own eyes, but he who heeds counsel is wise (Prov. 12:15)

We have already observed how William Wilberforce, the British politician who fought indefatigably against the evils of the slave trade, thought about entering the ministry after his conversion to Christ. What we did not divulge was why he gave up the idea. He chose to remain in politics because of counsel he received in 1785 from John Newton, the converted slave trader who is perhaps most famous as the author of the hymn, "Amazing Grace." John Newton was pastoring in London when Wilberforce appealed to him for direction: as a converted man, should he remain in the sensual, raucous environment of the political scene of his day? Newton replied with some timely advice: "It's hoped and believed that the Lord has raised you up for the good of the nation." Based on that recommendation, Wilberforce determined to make a difference in politics and set before himself the following agenda: "God Almighty has set before me two great objects, the suppression of the Slave Trade and the Reformation of Manners."[51] He overcame tremendous opposition during decades in the Parliament before finally seeing the slave trade abolished throughout the British Empire in 1807 and slavery itself in 1833.

BIBLICAL ADMONITIONS FROM PROVERBS TO SEEK COUNSEL

Wilberforce's example reminds us of the importance of seeking counsel in planning our lives God's way. Even secular analysts recognize the place of sound advice in decision-making. Benjamin Franklin is reported to have said, "He that won't be counseled can't be helped."

More importantly, Scripture repeatedly urges its readers to seek wise counsel. Proverbs is particularly full of such admonitions.

Where there is no counsel, the people fall; but in the multitude of **counselors** *there is safety* (11:14).

The way of a fool is right in his own eyes, but he who heeds **counsel** *is wise* (12:15).

Without counsel, plans go awry, but in the multitude of **counselors** *they are established* (15:22).

Listen to **counsel** *and receive instruction, that you may be wise in your latter days* (19:20).

For by wise **counsel** *you will wage your own war, and in a multitude of* **counselors** *there is safety* (24:6).

All of these verses insist on the value of seeking counsel. But for whom? What type of people seek counsel? The fool? The naïve? Listen to the words of the following verse:

A **wise man** *will hear and increase learning, and a* **man of understanding** *will attain wise counsel* (1:5).

We might initially think that wise people do not need advice but, surprisingly, they are the very ones who not only listen but actually profit from it!

I have, on occasion, given sage advice to children and received a very indifferent "I already know that" response. On the other hand, I have been in the presence of certain individuals who asked questions of *me* until it slowly dawned on me that they were the ones with the real knowledge of the issue under discussion. Wise people have learned to listen to the counsel of others.

BIBLICAL EXAMPLES OF GOOD AND BAD COUNSELORS

We do not, however, want to listen to just any kind of counselor. Scripture is clear that there are good and bad counselors.

Ahithophel has acquired a bad name because he followed Absalom in his rebellion, but he was an extremely skillful counselor. Consulting him for advice was like getting counsel from the mouth of God (2 Sam. 16:23). Even during Absalom's rebellion, the advice that Ahithophel gave him was better than the advice of Hushai, David's friend. (By "better" I do not mean more spiritual, but more suited to abet Absalom in his coup against his father.) Divine intervention alone made Absalom and the men of Israel abandon the "good counsel of Ahithophel" (17:14). Ahithophel knew his advice was better; and when it was not followed, he set his house in order and took his own life (v. 23).

King Rehoboam had access to both **older and younger counselors** (1 Kings 12:6-14). The sager advice was given by the elders who had served his father. They counseled him to listen to the concerns of the populace of Israel who were somewhat wearied with the heavy taxation and financial obligations during the reign of Solomon. The advice of Rehoboam's peers was blatantly harsh and, to our ears, perfectly suited to foment further rebellion against the house of David.

Perhaps one of the most unsung heroes of the Old Testament is **Jehoiada** the priest, the man who saved the house of David from certain extinction by rescuing Joash, the last-surviving son of Ahaziah, placing him on the throne, and ending the wicked reign of the usurper-queen Athaliah. Jehoiada went on to become Joash's counselor, and Joash did right all the time that Jehoiada instructed him (2 Kings 12:2).

Provocatively brief is the mention of **Zechariah**, the son of Shelemiah. He was the oldest of seven sons, and appointed gatekeeper of the north gate. Virtually nothing else is known about him except that he was a wise counselor (1 Chron. 26:14).

Sadly, King Ahaziah had wicked counselors (including **his own mother**) who led him astray and brought about his destruction (2 Chron. 22:3-4).

When faked overtures of friendship failed, those who opposed the rebuilding of the Temple hired **unprincipled counselors** and succeeded in halting the work for a dozen years or more (Ezra 4:1-5).

While wise people seek advice, they do not seek it from just anybody. Part of wisdom is the ability to discern wise counsel from its opposite.

THOSE WHO LISTENED TO OR DID NOT LISTEN TO ADVICE

Scripture also contains numerous examples of those who did or did not listen to advice. The consequences are often recorded so that we can see the importance of responding correctly. "He who can take advice is sometimes superior to him who can give it."[52]

David wisely heeded Abigail's advice not to take vengeance against her bad-mannered husband Nabal and blessed her for rescuing him from shedding blood carelessly (1 Sam. 25:33).

We have already noted that **Rehoboam** sought advice from two types of counselors. Sadly, he rejected the advice of his older counselors, followed the advice of his peers, and split the kingdom (1 Kings 12).

King Amaziah of Judah did not listen to the advice of God's prophet (2 Chron. 25:16-17); neither did **King Ahab** (1 Kings 22:26-27). Amaziah instead listened to imprudent counsel and ended up making a fool of himself in battle against King Joash of Israel. Ahab rejected the words of Micaiah, the true prophet of God, and opted instead to listen to prophetic charlatans more aligned with his thinking. Ahab discovered, however (as Matthew Henry puts it), that "no armour is of proof against the darts of divine vengeance."

Gedaliah, the governor appointed by Nebuchadnezzar to govern Judah after the fall of Jerusalem, should have listened to the advice of Johanan about the true motives and purpose of Ishmael. Johanan had somehow learned of the mutinous plan of Ishmael to reestablish the dynasty of David.[53] Gedaliah naively did not believe him and paid for his mistake with his life (Jer. 40:13-41:2).

Paul listened to Agabus' prophecy of his impending imprisonment in Jerusalem, acknowledged its probable truthfulness, but still felt compelled to continue his journey there (Acts 21:10-14; cf. 20:22-23). He did, however, heed the counsel of his nephew who had overheard the ambush plot against him, and he judiciously worked to prevent it (23:16-21).

WARNINGS FOR INSINCERE COUNSEL-SEEKERS

Remarkably, God sometimes uses advice to chastise a person for wrong doing. He caused **Absalom** to prefer the advice of Hushai over Ahithophel, even though Ahithophel's advice was more propitious (for Absalom).

Similarly, **Rehoboam's** decision to follow the harsher advice of his peers manifested the evil bent of his own heart (while simultaneously fulfilling God's decree to split the kingdom because of his father Solomon's idolatry).

We noted above how God used the flattering lies of false prophets to bring upon **King Ahab** the punishment his many sins deserved.

Examine the condition of your heart before seeking advice. To the wayward heart, advice can be a snare, a chastisement, and a peril.

Beware especially of a double-minded heart, one that seeks advice but has no real intention of following it up with obedience.

In the book of Jeremiah, **survivors of the Babylonian devastation** of Judah in 586 BC came to Jeremiah seeking his advice (42:1-2). Gedaliah, Judah's governor, had just been assassinated. The post-exilic community naturally feared the potentially violent reaction of Nebuchadnezzar to the murder of his personally appointed administrator, so they approached Jeremiah about the matter and committed themselves to obey whatever God said to him (42:5-6). However, when Jeremiah communicated to them God's will for them to remain in the land and His promise of no reprisal from Nebuchadnezzar, they denounced Jeremiah as a liar and proceeded to go to Egypt, the opposite of what God had just ordered (43:1-4).

A careful reader will observe that before they even approached Jeremiah for his advice (in chapter 42), they had already begun their journey toward Egypt: *And they departed and dwelt in the habitation of Chimham, which is near Bethlehem, as they* **went on their way to Egypt** (41:17). They had decided beforehand what they were going to do; they were just hoping that God would agree with them.

Tragically, they model impeccably the double-minded and unstable man that James speaks of in his epistle (1:8): *Let not that man suppose that he will receive anything from the Lord* (v. 7)!

Ahab's known duplicity of heart explains Micaiah's initial refusal to speak forthrightly to him regarding whether he should go to war against Syria (I Ki. 22:15). He knew that Ahab had no intention of obeying any advice he might give. Micaiah did finally give in and tell Ahab the truth: God had given permission for demonic spirits to fill Ahab's false prophets with lies in order to bring Ahab's life to an end (vv. 19-23). Instead of falling before Yahweh in repentance, Ahab ordered Micaiah to be imprisoned (v. 27)—as if that could somehow hinder the fulfillment of God's decree. Ahab proved himself to be the very double-minded man that Micaiah had diagnosed him to be.

BIBLICAL GUIDELINES FOR GENUINE COUNSEL-SEEKERS

So far in this chapter we have seen the importance the Scripture attaches to seeking counsel. We have also noted that truly wise people listen to advice, profit from it, and sort through their advisors carefully. In addition, the heart condition of the person seeking advice matters greatly. To the wayward or double minded in heart, advice-seeking may actually boomerang back on them and hurt rather than help them.

Using the passages we have considered above, we can draw up some biblical guidelines to follow when seeking advice.

(1) Seek (godly) counsel with the honest intention of obeying it.

A double-minded heart will either lead you to choose the wrong counselors or open you up to the possibility of being deceived by wrong advice. Prayerfully prepare your heart to obey the advice you are seeking.

(2) Approach more than just one counselor.

Because safety lies in a *multitude of counselors* (Prov. 11:14; 24:6), seek advice from more than just one counselor. A former pastor of mine recommends prayerfully choosing before the Lord two or three godly individuals from whom you can seek counsel and whom you think might be of genuine spiritual help to you. Then objectively lay your case out before them and consider strongly following the advice they give.

(3) Prioritize older, wiser advisors with a reputation for being good counselors.

Too often, we only forge friendships with people in our age group, and we lose the wisdom that friendship with an older person can bring. Your peers (like Rehoboam's) will probably not give you the best counsel (1 Kings 12:6-14).

In addition, prioritize the advice of those highly acclaimed in their fields of expertise. Latch onto a *Zechariah, the son of Shelemiah*, whenever you can find one (1 Chron. 26:14). Ahithophel ended very poorly, but he was a very astute counselor. In fact, he was the best in the entire Kingdom of Israel (2 Sam. 16:23). Who is the best counselor you know? You may actually want to ask that question more specifically. Who is the best counselor you know when it comes to the family? Who is the best counselor you know when it comes to handling finances?

Actually, the answer to the above questions may not be someone you know personally. Your best counselor might be a well-known author whose writings you can read or whose videos you can watch. Thanks to the existence of books and the internet, we can often gain access to some of the world's greatest (and godliest) minds when it comes to time management, financial planning, conflict resolution, organizational leadership, interpreting Scripture, overcoming addictions, and thousands of other topics.

(4) Listen to those who have your best interests at heart and who know you (or your situation) well.

Everyone needs a genuine friend who will give them "heartfelt counsel" (Prov. 27:9; NLT). Jonathan was such a friend to David, encouraging and supporting him even though he knew David's survival would cost him his father's throne (1 Sam. 23:16-18). Gedaliah foolishly overlooked the advice of a man (Johanan) who was on his side (Jer. 40:14). Do not underrate advice from a heart that sincerely cares for you, even if you do not agree with the advice initially. Probe the person for more details; ascertain the reason for their concerns. *Do not be wise in your own opinion* (Rom. 12:16).

Similarly, those who know you best will often give you the best counsel. Sometimes, we seek counselors from afar, perhaps because it seems safer to air our deepest struggles with a perfect stranger. However, someone who does not know you well will often only be able to give you general advice. Those closest to you or the situation can be more specific (and, often, more accurate).

Do not undervalue the advice of a mother or father just because they are unsaved. They may not know the Lord, but they know you well and (typically) have your best interests at heart. Moses wisely followed the advice of his father-in-law Jethro, a brand-new believer in the God of Israel. Jethro may not have had as deep of a relationship with Yahweh as Moses had, but the depth of his wisdom about Moses' need to delegate the task of leading over two million people is apparent (Exodus 18:10-24).

(5) Heed those committed to declaring to you God's words (whether you like it or not).

We often know when the advice we are receiving is biblical and exactly what God wanted us to hear. Ahab surely had a hunch that Micaiah was right when he predicted his death (why else did Ahab disguise himself in the battle that ensued?), but he felt he could maneuver his way around the prophecy. Don't be like Ahab. If God gives you a "Micaiah," whose straight-speaking makes you uncomfortable, praise God for him (or her) and prepare your ears and heart to hear. Unfortunately, pride, selfish desire, personality conflict, a desire not to appear wrong, and a variety of other factors may keep us from responding the way we should.

Jeremiah is another example (like Micaiah) of a man who would not withhold, twist, or misrepresent what God had said. Surely the post-exilic community of his day knew what kind of man he was! Yet they turned on him because they did not like what he said (at God's behest). As we have already seen, it went against their pre-set plans.

(6) Not all counsel to avoid danger is necessarily God's will.

Agabus (and others) were correct in foreseeing imprisonment for Paul in Jerusalem. What they could not have known was that such imprisonment was part of God's plan for Paul. Paul felt constrained in his spirit to go to Rome, and his imprisonment in Jerusalem was actually God's providential means of sending Paul there (Acts 19:21; 23:11). We should listen to the counsel of others when they warn of impending danger, but ultimately we must obey whatever God tells us to do. It is not always God's will for a believer to avoid danger.

In 2015, I was invited to speak at a conference in the province of Zamboanga on the island of Mindanao. Zamboanga is a hotbed of Islamic terrorism and unrest, and foreigners are generally advised to avoid it. Those in Manila who heard of the invitation counseled against my going. I opted to follow the advice of the local Zamboanga pastors who had invited me since they were closest to the situation. As it turned out, they were right. Pagadian City, where I was invited to speak, has a large Philippines military camp nearby and is considered fairly safe (as long as you stay in the city). Admittedly, the pastors provided a bodyguard at all times—I was never alone, not even when I was asleep.

HEEDING BIBLICAL ADVICE ADVANCES GOD'S KINGDOM

At the end of the day, the best thing about being a person who seeks and listens to biblical counsel is that God is glorified and His kingdom benefits. R. G. LeTourneau was a gifted inventor of large earth-moving equipment, who designed over fifty percent of the earth-moving machines used in World War II. LeTourneau surrendered to Christ as a young man and considered going into full-time Christian service. After all, how else does a Christian show his surrender to his Lord? His pastor, however, counseled him that "God needs business men [sic] as well as missionaries."[54] That advice led LeTourneau to continue in his business and to make God his business partner. LeTourneau decided that he and God would split the business profit as follows: God would get ninety percent; he would receive the remaining ten percent. Millions of dollars were given to the Lord's work as a result of a young inventor willing to listen to spiritually-minded counsel.

‹ 12 ›

When You Are Not Sure What to Do

It is not in man who walks to direct his own steps (Jer. 10:23)

In his poem "The Road Not Taken," Robert Frost tells of a traveler who stood at the fork where "two roads diverged in a yellow wood." The traveler realized he could not take both paths and eventually decided for the "one less traveled by," hoping against hope that he might have a second chance to try the other pathway someday.

We all know what it is to stand at a fork in the road of our life and wonder what we ought to do. You may, in fact, have really worked to apply the kinds of principles spelled out in a book like this: You have bowed before Jesus as the Son of God and embarked on the exciting journey of being His disciple. You have ransacked the Bible for principles that apply to your situation. You have prayed for wisdom in assessing the opportunities that lie open before you. You have asked advice from three of the godliest people you know.

Nevertheless, you are still not sure what to do. Moreover, your three counselors have given you three different answers, and you have reached the point of potentially shrugging your shoulders and choosing an option merely because it is "less traveled." What now?

First, know you that you are not alone. Your lack of definite direction is not necessarily an indication that something is wrong with you or that God has abandoned you. As we have noted in a previous chapter, many godly servants of the Lord, including the Apostle Paul, faced times when they did not know for sure what they were supposed to do. Second, consider the following principles that may help you in times of uncertainty or befuddlement.

(1) Focus on doing what you know is God's will for you today.

Sometimes we neglect current duties due to a fixation on the future. Over one hundred Christian books have been written on the subject of God's will because, in part, people are frustrated by their current life situation and hope that the future holds something more enchanting— the fabled pot of gold at the end of the rainbow.

In reality, God's will is more *present* than future. Ecclesiastes warns us against pursuing the exotic as a panacea for the dissatisfaction in life that we are experiencing now. Solomon tried all of that—on a grander scale than almost any of us could ever afford—and concluded (to use New Testament terminology) that *godliness* **with contentment** *is great gain* (1 Tim. 6:6).

Gerald Sittser makes a compelling argument about the importance of the everyday, the mundane, and the ordinary.[55] We are, he says, too often like children who want to do something special on Mother's Day (like serve mom breakfast in bed), but who do not want to take out the trash every day.

Similarly, we are eager to find and do the grandiose plan that God has for us in the future, forgetting that our daily habits, relationships, convictions, and routines *are* the preparation for the future. God has made life routine "because routine itself is like a laboratory in which God grows us up. God is the scientist; we are the experiment…. It is doing the little things every day that puts us on a trajectory of fulfilling the will of God."[56] We all want God to guide us into a stellar future career but are slow to apply ourselves to our studies now. We expect God to show us whom we should marry but make no (or little) present effort to better our interpersonal skills. Obeying God today is your preparation for doing His will tomorrow.

(2) Do not worry or borrow trouble from tomorrow.

Ask yourself whether your decision is one that you need to make right now. Sometimes we get all bent out of shape over something that we do not even need to know yet. *Sufficient for today is the evil thereof* (Matt. 6:34). Tomorrow will take care of itself. If you are not sure yet what you should do, it may be that you do not need to know yet. Plan further. Pray more. Seek out another counselor. Go back through the relevant Scripture passages again. Wait. More times than not, when you need to know, God will be there to point the way.

Furthermore, worry about the future may actually keep you from reaching the "sweet spot"[57] in life where your uniqueness intersects with the kingdom of God. The same passage that exhorts us to seek first God's kingdom and righteousness forbids us to worry (Matt. 6:25-34). Why? Too many believers have let worry about tomorrow—and how they will physically survive in it—keep them from what they knew God was telling them to do today. Instead of focusing first on your needed daily provision, seek first His kingdom and His righteousness. Make the latter *your* concern, and He will make the former *His*!

(3) Rest confident that God answers every prayer offered in Jesus' name.

Too often we view prayer the way a basketball player views his three-point shooting percentage or a baseball player his batting average. "I get about 35% of my prayers answered." "Really?," your somewhat boastful friend replies, "I am batting about .500 in my prayer life."

153

When Jesus taught His disciples to pray, He gave great encouragements to ask: *Continue asking and it shall be given to you; be seeking and you shall find* (Luke 11:9; my translation). God wants us to ask, to be persistent about asking, and to expect Him to answer. My pastor used to remind us: "When you pray, what happens is God's will!" In other words, if you pray for the Lord to open a certain door and He does not, then that is His answer. If the door on a certain relationship closes, that is God. If He does not take away the cancer, that was His will, at least for now. It may not have been the answer you wanted, but it is still an answer.

We must believe that our prayers are heard and that the results that follow are God's answers to those prayers. Of course, this assumes that we are adhering to God's directives for prayer, especially as it relates to praying in Jesus' name. Jesus, in His final instructions to His disciples before His crucifixion, reiterated to them the effectiveness of prayer in His name.

And whatever you ask **in My name***, that I will do, that the Father may be glorified in the Son. If you ask anything* **in My name***, I will do it* (John 14:13-14).

You did not choose Me, but I chose you and appointed you that you should go and bear fruit, and that your fruit should remain, that whatever you ask the Father **in My name** *He may give you* (15:16).

And in that day you will ask Me nothing. Most assuredly, I say to you, whatever you ask the Father **in My name** *He will give you. Until now you have asked nothing* **in My name***. Ask, and you will receive, that your joy may be full . . . . In that day you will ask* **in My name***, and I do not say to you that I shall pray the Father for you* (16:23-24, 26).

Every prayer offered in His name will be answered. Praying in Jesus' name, however, is not just tacking on His name at the end of a prayer—a signal of sorts that the prayer is almost over (which is the way my four-year-old twin boys view it). Rather, praying in Jesus' name is praying in accordance with His mission, His will, and His purposes.

Praying in Jesus' name is asking for what Jesus would ask for in your situation.

Picture prayer like writing a check. You make out the check to the Father. (He is our primary addressee in prayer.) The check amount is the petition which we have asked for. Praying in Jesus' name is asking Jesus to sign the check—to sign off on your petition. This ought to give a heightened seriousness to the way we pray. Would Jesus really "sign" the petition you just offered up? Is it really according to His will? Praying in Jesus' name presupposes that we are filled with Jesus' words and are praying accordingly.

*If you abide in Me, and **My words abide in you**, ask whatever you wish, and it shall be done for you* (John 15:7; NASB).

We look at the life of George Müller (whom we have mentioned before) and envy all his answers to prayer.

Need bread? The local baker cannot rest or sleep until he prepares three batches and brings it to him.

Out of milk? A milk cart breaks down in front of the orphanage.

We wish it worked that way for us. We forget that Müller was a man who through daily and prolonged saturation of himself with Scripture knew the mind of God and, therefore, prayed according to the will of God. Abiding in Jesus' words is essential to praying in Jesus' name.

Prayer, by the way, is not just a psychological crutch to offload our frustrations. God really does answer prayer. How an absolutely sovereign God can also be experienced by His people as *You who hear prayer* (Psa. 65:2) is incomprehensible, but the Bible reveals both traits to be true of Him. God has factored believing prayer into His sovereign plans. We find instances in Scripture where God states His will and then promptly "reverses" it when someone prays. For example, God declares that He will destroy Israel but then does not when Moses prays (Exod. 32:9-14). God says that Hezekiah will die but then heals him when he prays (2 Kings 20:1-5).

Did God change His mind? Does God's will fluctuate? Is He whimsical? Or limited in knowledge? Preposterous nonsense! *God is not a man...that He should repent* (Num. 23:19). God revealed His initial "decision" (to destroy Israel or for Hezekiah to die) and then disclosed His "reversal" in order to reveal how prayer is an essential part of His working. If Hezekiah had not prayed, he would have died. If Moses had not prayed, Israel would have been zapped out of existence. That's how effective prayer is.

The hymn writer verbalized it this way:

> He will answer every prayer,
> He will answer every prayer,
> Go to Him in faith believing,
> He will answer every prayer.
> (Mary Bernstecher, "He Will Answer Every Prayer")

Good thing that God answers every prayer because He commands us to pray about everything.

Do not be anxious about anything. Instead, in every situation, through prayer and petition with thanksgiving, tell your requests to God (Phil. 4:6; NET).

Muslims pride themselves on praying five times a day. A surrendered Christian does not even come close to praying a mere five times a day: he (or she) prays without ceasing (1 Thess. 5:17), bringing all of his worries, intercessions, needs, sins, and burdens to the Lord constantly. *Casting **all** your care upon Him, for He cares for you* (I Peter 5:7). If your burdens are anything like mine, you are in prayer all day and even sometimes in the middle of the night.

(4) Take comfort in the prayers of the Holy Spirit for you.

Romans 8:26-27 connects knowing God's will with the subject of prayer, specifically the role of the Holy Spirit in interceding for us in times of personal distress.[58]

Likewise the Spirit also helps in our weaknesses. For we do not know what we should pray for as we ought, but the Spirit Himself makes intercession for us with groanings which cannot be uttered. Now He who searches the hearts knows what the mind of the Spirit is, because He makes intercession for the saints according to the will of God.

The word *will* (in the phrase *will of God*) is not actually in the Greek text of verse 27; but the idea is, and virtually all translations pick it up. In the context of our suffering, verse 26 concedes that we do not always know how to pray or what to pray for. We are, in fact, sometimes genuinely bewildered by the circumstance facing us, the advice that we are receiving, or by the options that are multiplying before us.

Here is where this passage provides very comforting news: when we are at a loss as to what to pray, we gain the Spirit as our Intercessor. He picks up, so to speak, where we leave off. And because He is God, He prays for us *according to the will of God* (v. 27). This ought to bring us great solace in times of genuine bewilderment when the heavens seem silent and our pathway completely fogged over. He is praying for you according to the will of God, and because of who He is, you are not likely to miss the way. In fact, these two verses lay the groundwork for the passage we often quote so casually: *all things work together for good to them that love God . . .* (v. 28). Verse 28 is true because of what the Holy Spirit is doing in verses 26-27.

(5) Do what is in your heart to do for the Lord.

A previous chapter alluded to the advice of Nathan the prophet to David, when he expressed his desire to build a house for his God: *"Go, do all that is in your heart, for the LORD is with you"* (2 Sam. 7:3). David's life had the stamp of one walking with God, his motive for building a Temple was biblical, and his purpose was laudable. So Nathan gave him an initial green light.

For a surrendered believer, the starting point for doing God's will is often the *desires of his or her heart* because those desires have come from

God (Psa. 37:4). Ask yourself, "What do I most want to do for the Lord?" Through your desires (again, as a believer genuinely seeking to plan his or her life God's way), God is often directing your path. "If you are the right you, you can follow your desires and you will fulfill His will."[59]

Nehemiah's remarkable repair of Jerusalem's walls in only fifty-two days began when he heard the report of its broken-down condition. The burden to help grew as he nurtured it with prayer, realized it was a task within the scope of his abilities, and saw the Lord grant him favor with King Artaxerxes (Neh. 1:3-4, 11; 2:8). Fixing Jerusalem's walls (and resolving some of its other problems) fulfilled the desire of Nehemiah's heart.

King Josiah purged all idolatry from his kingdom and from all the shrines of the former Northern Kingdom. Where did the desire to do that come from? Josiah's reading of Scripture convinced him of God's hatred for idolatry, and his position as king rendered him the fitting candidate to do something about it (2 Kings 22:11-13; 23:1-20) .

Similarly, ask yourself questions like the following: What am I gifted to do? What most fits my personality? My training? My position in life? Does anything in my background indicate what God has been preparing me to do? What was I made to do? If I could do anything for God, what would I choose?

Author-pastor John MacArthur tells the story of counseling a man who was unsure of God's will for him. He asked the man, "What do you want to do?" The man's reply was that since he was a French-speaking Jew, he wanted to reach other French-speaking Jews in France. MacArthur counseled him, "Get moving!" The man ended up reaching French-speaking Jews—in Canada.[60] He had the right idea, but the wrong place. God led him to the right place as he followed the desires that God had put in his heart.

(6) Take a risk and try.

Too often we hesitate to step out by faith to do what is in our hearts because we fear failure. Given the risks involved in almost any endeavor and the unknowns that could so easily sink it, we waste our lives in the valley of indecision and inactivity. Perhaps this is truer for men than women. Men fear failure more than almost anything else: to blunder or be ridiculed or laughed at is just not worth the risk of trying.

Ecclesiastes 11:1-6 reminds us that life is a hazardous venture full of unknowns. Whatever the exact point of the imagery in verses 1-2, the overall message is clear: if you do not take a calculated risk, you will certainly not experience the benefits. Because we do not know what kind of disasters lie ahead, we should multiply our strategies and not put all our eggs in one basket (v. 2). We cannot control the clouds or the direction a tree in a forest will fall (v. 3). If you wait for perfect circumstances, you will end up doing nothing (v. 4).

No man knows everything about how God works (v. 5). That is a scary admission that sends some into lifelong passivity. Will her parents say "yes"? Will the restaurant I want to open boom like Chick-fil-A? Will my pioneer church plant flourish? Will my book sell if I write it? Our tendency is to wait to act until assured of the positive outcome of our plans. God, however, does not typically work by giving us advance guarantees. We want control of the future (or at least a knowledge of what will happen in it). God wants immediate obedience as we trust Him about future consequences. *We walk by faith, not by sight* (2 Cor. 5:7).

Precisely because we do not (and cannot) know in advance what will prosper, we should be more diligent.

In the morning sow your seed, and in the evening do not withhold your hand; for you do not know which will prosper, either this or that, or whether both alike will be good (Ecc. 11:6).

Try in the morning. Try again in the evening. Work the whole day if necessary. Exhaust all of your options. You cannot predict *which will prosper...or whether both alike will be good*, so take a risk and try!

Esther did not have complete assurance that she would succeed before King Ahasuerus. Mordecai had reminded her of her providential position as queen and the duty implicit upon her to go before the king (Est. 4:14). Prayerfully, she accepted the risk and tried. She knew what she should do for her people, but she did not know what the result of her actions would be (v. 16).

Gideon was far more fortunate than Esther in that God did guarantee the outcome of his battle with the Midianites. Gideon had a different problem. In spite of the promise he had been given (Judges 6:14-16) and the subsequent sign he had received (vv. 17-23), he wanted more confirmation. First he asked for a wet fleece, then a dry fleece (vv. 36-40). Even after all his fleece-wrangling, God knew the fear still needlessly embedded in Gideon's heart and gave him yet another proof (7:9-14). Only after that final sign did Gideon bow in confident worship (v. 15). The story of Gideon reminds us to ask ourselves, "Why am I so fearful?" or "Should I be so fearful?" Sometimes we, like him, are afraid to obey clear commands of God and claim His promises, until some kind of supernatural sign has bolstered our chances of success (or, at least, our confidence). Far better is to derive all our confidence from God's promises! Determine what God has commanded you to do, and then obey it.

Have I not commanded you? Be strong and of good courage; do not be afraid, nor be dismayed, for the LORD your God is with you wherever you go (Josh. 1:9).

In summary, too many believers never get around to doing anything because they are never certain enough of the outcome. They want an advance guarantee before proceeding, and they spend their whole life waiting for just the right moment. Excuses are not hard to come by: "It might rain" or "the clouds look kind of dark" (Ecc. 11:4); or, if either of those fails, *there is a lion outside* (Prov. 22:13). (Try that on your boss sometime when you don't feel like going to work.) Sadly, the excuses of the lazy or the fearful multiply as the precious moments of their life slip past unused, untried, and un-invested. Is this not partially the lesson from the parable of the talents (Matt. 25:14-30)? The servant given one talent did not want to fail his master, so he did nothing. Better to have done something—even to have flopped completely—than to have done nothing at all.

(7) Work your plans, knowing that God is ordering your steps.

Ultimately, we can "take a risk and try" because of assurances like this: *The steps of a good man are ordered by the LORD, and He delights in his way* (Psa. 37:23). Work your plans knowing that God is ordering your steps.

Paul did not wait around until he had discerned God's will in all its particulars. He laid plans, and then he did what was in his hand to do at the time. When he wrote the book of Romans, for example, he had never been to Rome. He desired to go and fellowship with the believers there (Rom. 1:11; 15:23). He also saw a visit there as a stepping stone for his eventual plan to evangelize Spain (15:24), but he lacked the complete assurance that it was God's will for him to go to Rome (1:10). Nonetheless, he laid his plans to go and submitted the actual execution of those plans to the Lord whom he knew would order (or re-order) his steps (15:28). *A man's heart plans his way, but the LORD directs his steps* (Prov. 16:9). You will never be able to fully understand your way because your *steps are of the Lord* (20:24).

SOMEWHERE BETWEEN PANIC AND PASSIVITY

Do not be so paranoid of somehow messing up God's plan for you that you do nothing. If God can work with stubborn Jonah, outspoken Peter, and doubting Thomas, He can certainly handle you! You may fall, but you will never be *utterly cast down* (Psa. 37:24).

Frankly, a fully surrendered and Spirit-filled believer is not likely to miss God's will for his or her life. Do not picture the quest for God's will as a real-life edition of the Tom & Jerry Show—a lifelong, frustrating cat-and-mouse hunt, where the mouse barely but consistently eludes the cat. The will of God is not so much something you find as something that finds you. It is not something you discover in the future so much as something you are doing right now; not a video to watch in advance, but a drama you are living out in the present. A sovereign, omnipotent but caring God directs your every movement, scene by scene.

After walking with the Lord for sixty-nine years, George Müller uttered the following testimony:

> I never remember in all my Christian course . . . that I ever sincerely and patiently sought to know the will of God by the *teaching of the Holy Ghost*, through the *instrumentality of the Word of God,* but I have been always directed rightly.

Yes, you should feel an appropriate concern, even anxiety, to do what is right: *Work out your salvation with* **fear and trembling** (Phil. 2:12). Then connect the next verse: *for* **it is God** *who is working in you to be willing and to be doing of His good pleasure* (v. 13). You were created in Christ Jesus unto good works that God prepared for you from eternity past (Eph. 2:10). Do you really think that if you conscientiously walk with Him, God will let you stray from those works? His glory—around which the entire universe and beyond revolves—is at stake.

You are not like a fisherman battered by a storm, with no idea which way land is, frantically rowing his boat in hopes that he will somehow find it. Your Helmsman is at the wheel! If you cling to Him, you will not be lost at sea!

◀ **13** ▶

Trapped by the Past?

Thus says the LORD: ". . . this thing is from Me" (2 Chron. 11:4)

Your past does not define you; it prepares you." My wife repeated the words as we flashed by the billboard at interstate speed.

The statement reminded me of the life of Mary Slessor, missionary to Calabar, West Africa. Born to Scottish parents, Mary faced a childhood that pitted a devout mother against an alcoholic father. The healthy spiritual influence of her mother could not negate the physical consequences of her father's destructive addiction. Poverty stalked the family. Hunger became a reality. So did anger, violence, and abuse. Mary was forced to work instead of attending school. Whatever education she received was squeezed in after hours of drudgery as a textile-mill factory worker.

The sad threads of Mary's childhood form a tapestry similar to that woven in the lives of many others. These threads too often produce a hopeless feeling of being trapped by the past.

We all have circumstances that we wish we could change. For some people, however, their scarred past becomes a real hurdle (in their thinking) to doing the will of God in the present. They feel trapped in a life that, like a deck of cards, has been stacked against them. Even more frustrating is when it is because of somebody else's missteps.

I have a friend in the Philippines who was privileged with access to quality private education until his father gambled and drank away the family's money. His dream of attending one of the most elite colleges in the Philippines vaporized because of his dad's vices and the family's resulting inability to meet the tuition demands. His only choice was to attend a less prestigious college.

Maybe you feel like your future has been similarly sabotaged. Your parents or your boss or your spouse or a sibling did you wrong, and the brunt of the negative consequences has fallen on you. For all practical purposes—as you see it—your life has been damaged beyond repair.

Does God's Word give any guidance in situations like these? Did anyone else in Scripture face a situation where they had to overcome a past they did not choose?

1 Kings 11-12 informs us that King Solomon, rich and wise almost beyond imagination, did the unthinkable and turned from the true God to the idols of his foreign wives. As a consequence, God decreed the division of the Kingdom of Israel. Ten tribes would be given to a rebel Ephraimite leader by the name of Jeroboam.

But here's the rub: God willed the division to take place during the days of Rehoboam (11:12). In other words, the kingdom would divide during *Rehoboam's* reign because of sins that his father *Solomon* had committed. Rehoboam was trapped in a negative situation beyond his control and, worse yet, not of his own doing. Does that sound fair?

Second Chronicles 11-12 records Rehoboam's responses—some good, some bad—to the situation in which he found himself. His responses and the truths God was teaching him throughout can help guide others who feel trapped in the present by a past beyond their control.

(1) God is at work in all of our circumstances

Rehoboam's first response was that of any king: to take back what was formerly his. He gathered an army of 180,000 men in order to reclaim the kingdom from the hand of Jeroboam (2 Chron. 11:1). However, when he received word from the prophet that what had transpired was from the hand of God, he nobly refrained from going against the enemy kingdom. He instead accepted his current situation as from the Lord—*this thing is from me* (vv. 2-4).

Like Rehoboam, we also need to accept our inherited negative circumstances as from the Lord! Regardless of how you ended up in your current situation, ultimately *this thing is done of God*. God does not cause wicked men to do evil, but God is sovereign even over their wicked actions, and He makes the *wrath of man to praise Him* (Psa. 76:10).

When Jesus was here on earth, He made the startling claim that He was "Lord of the Sabbath." This claim baffled the Pharisees of His day and was one that they could not accept. Similarly, some people struggle with the idea that God is Lord of all their circumstances. This, however, is where we must start when grappling with an unsavory past: by bowing the knee in submission before the God who has ordered all of our circumstances.

Joseph was sold into slavery in Egypt due to the malice of his older brothers (Gen. 37:1-28). Yet twice Joseph acknowledges that what his brothers intended for evil, God meant for good (45:5-8; 50:20). In fact, he goes so far as to say that they did not send him to Egypt; God did (45:8). Joseph realized that God was at work in all his circumstances.

Perhaps you too have been victimized. Evil actions perpetrated against you without your consent or desire have left you with scars or other after-effects that are far from pleasant. Embrace the God who is orchestrating even your ugly circumstances into a symphony of harmony and praise.

Mary Slessor—to return to our earlier story—grew to understand this. As an adult, God placed her in Africa (in modern-day Nigeria) where she ministered among warring tribes who often drank themselves into a state of enraged inebriation and then set off on the war path. Mary bravely stood her ground against these rum-possessed men. Living with an alcoholic father had been God's school to train her for her future kingdom assignment. Even in the undesirable circumstances of her growing-up years, God was at work.

God is also in control of accidents that alter our entire lives. Seemingly random things like casting lots fall under His jurisdiction.

The lot is cast into the lap, but its every decision is from the LORD (Prov. 16:33).

When someone is inadvertently killed by a wayward stone, a flying axe head, or some other unforeseen calamity, Scripture refers to it as *God* delivering that person into the hand of the other.

*However, if he did not lie in wait, but **God** delivered him into his hand, then I will appoint for you a place where he may flee* (Exod. 21:13).

Humanly, it may be an accident; but from heaven's perspective, a larger purpose is at work in the tragic and unforeseen mishap.

We also, like Rehoboam, need to accept that our circumstances come from the Lord. The events of our lives are part of a larger script. One scene may be more chaotic than another, but when the final act has been played out and the curtain has fallen for the last time, a sense of order and even grandeur will fill every heavenly and earthly onlooker.

(2) God gives us ample opportunity to do good in our present circumstances

Rehoboam's next response, after pulling back from his initial desire to roast Jeroboam over an open fire, was to rebuild the fifteen cities listed in 2 Chronicles 11:5-12. Most Christians have heard of the town of Bethlehem, but what about the fourteen other cities listed in these verses? These cities are all in Judah, the part of the kingdom that still belonged to Rehoboam. Apparently, rather than fret about what he did not have, Rehoboam set himself to improve what he did have. He built cities for defense—including Bethlehem, where the Messiah would be born—and otherwise massively improved his military readiness. He made the most of his present circumstances. We need to do the same.

Whatever your hand finds to do, do it with your might; for there is no work or device or knowledge or wisdom in the grave where you are going (Ecc. 9:10).

Rather than be frustrated about what we do not have—the magnificent future stolen from your grasp by a bungling father or an envious sibling—make the best of what you do have. Joseph could have spent his years in Egypt whining about what could have been. After all, it was not exactly his fault that he was there. Instead, he rolled up his sleeves and went to work in the circumstances where God had put him.

Two applications flow naturally out of the truth that *God gives us ample opportunity to do good in our present circumstances.* The first is that probably none of us lacks for things to do, even if we are under the most limiting of circumstances. Most of us fall exhausted into bed at night, clutching an unfinished to-do list. Should we really complain because we do not have more opportunities?

Second, sometimes it is in our limiting circumstances that we find the sovereignly-specific works which God prepared for us before the world began (Eph. 2:10). Author and inspirational speaker Joni Eareckson Tada has become a household name. She would probably be largely unknown and not nearly as widely used of God if she had not been paralyzed as a teenager in a swimming accident. No one would ask for such circumstances, but it was *because of* them that she has become a blessing to so many.

Because our work as missionaries is very itinerant in nature, our family does a lot of travel by car. One of our children's favorite pastimes to help whittle the time away is to listen to "Patch the Pirate," a series of children's musical dramas that feature the heroic exploits of "Captain Patch" and his band of sailors. Along the way, wholesome biblical principles are regularly injected.

Ron Hamilton launched into his shiver-me-timbers career as a pirate when cancer destroyed his right eye and resulted in a pirate-like eye patch. Where would he be without that cancer? He certainly would not be sailing around the world in the Jolly Roger, solving mysteries, cracking criminal cases, and teaching truth to children all over the world.

Paul similarly was "blessed" with a thorn in the flesh that hindered and limited him. His infirmity kept him dependent on the grace of God and, therefore, perpetually useful for God's kingdom.

And lest I should be exalted above measure by the abundance of the revelations, a thorn in the flesh was given to me, a messenger of Satan to buffet me, lest I be exalted above measure. Concerning this thing I pleaded with the Lord three times that it might depart from me. And He said to me, "My grace is sufficient for you, for My strength is made perfect in weakness" (2 Cor. 12:7-9a).

(3) God rewards any believer who will truly seek Him

Rehoboam's commendable responses to his circumstances were seen and rewarded by God. Rehoboam's kingdom was smaller than his father's, to be sure, but God found other ways of rewarding and encouraging Rehoboam. Priests and Levites, upset with Jeroboam's counterfeit worship in the newly-formed Northern Kingdom, moved to Rehoboam's Southern Kingdom and strengthened it, bringing a time of national security and stability (2 Chron. 11:13-17). Rehoboam saw his family grow (vv. 18-21), his children placed in positions of authority in the kingdom (vv. 22-23a), and their families established (v. 23b). These were God's rewards.

Some people feel that they are living under a curse because their parents did something wrong or because of some other event beyond their control. Verses like Exodus 20:5, which asserts the consequence for breaking the Second Commandment's prohibition against making idols for worship, seem to support their case:

For I, the LORD your God, am a jealous God, visiting the iniquity of the fathers on the children to the third and fourth generations of those who hate Me.

In the case of idolatrous worship, God will punish the children for the sins of their fathers, but the punishment only falls upon the future generations of those who *continue* to hate the Lord. In other words, repentance breaks the cycle of judgment. How else can you explain God's wonderful promises to Abraham? Abraham's own father Terah was an idolater (Josh. 24:2), and yet look at the blessing that came out of Abraham's life!

God *is a rewarder of them that diligently seek him* (Heb. 11:6). Shake off the drooping shoulders and furrowed brow, walk with God, and enjoy the life He has for you. Do not compare it with others or with your forefathers, but rejoice in it for what it is. God's best rewards are not the glamour and glitz of stardom. God's best rewards are found in the daily pursuit of His will: work that you enjoy and that satisfies, a wife in your youth, and provision exactly suited to you and your tastes (Ecc. 9:7-9). These, the preacher of Ecclesiastes assures us, are gifts from God (3:13; 5:19).

(4) Your own sinful heart [not your past] is what will most limit you

Unfortunately, the story of Rehoboam does not have a Disney ending. As it turns out, Rehoboam's greatest problem was not his father's sin, the division of the kingdom, or his rival, King Jeroboam. Rehoboam's biggest problem was his own heart.

*And he did evil because **he did not set his heart** to seek the LORD* (2 Chron. 12:14).

Rehoboam's three years of doing right were a parenthesis in a life otherwise dominated by ungodly behavior. A spiritual fickleness characterized him that a careful observer would have noticed early on: he was willing to listen to his peers instead of the seasoned older men who had counseled his father (10:6-15). One begins to see that although God decreed the division of the kingdom because of his father's sins, Rehoboam himself was not exactly free of wrong doing. He had never firmly resolved in his heart that he would follow the Lord.

Similarly, our biggest problem is not our circumstances. It is not our parents or their failures. It is not the economy or our president, nor is it our pathetic salary or crowded living conditions. Our biggest problem is our heart! We may be so focused on our circumstances or perceived wrongs inherited from our fathers that we fail to realize that the biggest problems in our lives are self-inflicted. Esau's biggest problem, for example, was not his scheming brother, Jacob, but his own lack of spiritual desire (Heb. 12:16). The author of Hebrews issues a warning to his readers that still rings true today: *Beware lest there be in any one of you an evil, unbelieving heart, leading you to fall away from the living God* (3:12).

Jonathan, the courageous son of King Saul, exemplifies a man who responded correctly to adverse circumstances. Jonathan was a godly man, a valiant warrior, and a loyal friend of David's. Jonathan had every right, humanly speaking, to be the next king of Israel. No recorded blemish stains his life. However, because of his father's refusal to obey, God decreed that Saul's royal line be cut off, and that David, instead, become the next king of Israel.

Jonathan accepted these circumstances as from the Lord. In fact, on one occasion he told David, *you shall be the next king of Israel, and I will be next to you* (1 Sam. 23:17). Jonathan recognized that David was God's choice to be the next king and resigned himself to it willingly, even offering to assist David in the role that rightfully was his own.

How about you? Can you trust God that the tragedies in your past might be part of a larger plan?

OUR GRAND ARTIST

Recently, I was watching my sister-in-law tutor six children in basic painting. One child had drawn tree trunks in the foreground that were far too thick in comparison to the spindly-looking ones in the background. To my unpracticed eye, the scene was unsalvageable. Not to my sister-in-law's. When I came back later, she had thickened the trunks of the other trees and brought everything back into harmony. A little different from the child's original design? Sure! Still beautiful? Remarkably so!

This is like the work of the Grand Artist in our lives. A blotch or a smear, an irremediable stain can, under His touch, be so lovingly incorporated into the overall design of our lives that the final picture is actually more beautiful, more truly serviceable, than our original would ever have been. Like Mary Slessor's. Like Joni Eareckson Tada's. Like Ron Hamilton's.

Like yours.

Scarred by the past? Don't let it trap you. Move forward, and begin planning your life God's way.

‹ 14 ›

Remedy for Past Failure

O LORD, Pardon my iniquity, for it is great (Psa. 25:11)

Perhaps as you have worked through the preceding chapters of this book, your failures have so filled your vision that you do not see much point in even trying anymore. You agree with David, *my sin is always before me* (Psa. 51:3). Maybe reading this book has had the unintended effect of discouraging you. Your sins have created so many tangles in your life that to extricate yourself seems about as possible as pinning Jell-O to the wall with an icepick.

A few years ago, Psalm 25 came alive to me in a way it never had before, and it has become my "go-to" psalm in times when I have sinned against the Lord. Interweaving as it does the themes of guidance, forgiveness, trouble, and confidence (in God), it provides great comfort for those who have miserably failed, feel their guilt, and face potential consequences because of their actions. Its psalm title identifies David as the author but provides no details as to the predicament that birthed it. Clearly, he is in trouble and there are enough references to sin and guilt for us to conjecture that some connection exists between his trouble and his sins.

Psalm 25 defies any effort to outline it tidily. One reason is that it is a Hebrew acrostic. That is, each verse begins with a successive letter of the Hebrew alphabet (which is why the psalm has 22 verses).[61] Since an acrostic has its own built-in organizational principle, it does not break down easily into the nifty outline that we modern readers find so attractive. In addition, Psalm 25 is a lament, a type of psalm that contains a cry for help in a time of crisis. Lament psalms are notoriously difficult to outline because they are the outpouring of unorganized emotion. Nevertheless, tracing the general movements of David's prayer yields the following rough sketch:

> **Vv. 1-3:** Opening cry for help with an expression of confidence

> **Vv. 4-7:** Multiple petitions, divided neatly between requests for guidance and **forgiveness**

> **Vv. 8-15:** With the exception of one plea for **forgiveness** (v. 11), expressions of confidence that God will provide the guidance, favor, and deliverance requested

> **Vv. 16-21:** More petitions, one for **forgiveness** (v. 18) but mostly asking God to see the author's troubles and deliver him

> **V. 22:** Concluding intercession for the nation as a whole

Even at the risk of being a bit verbally cumbersome in my sketch above, I have attempted to show how request for pardon punctuates the psalm in order to underscore that this psalm is not offered from the lips of one confessing his own integrity. Rather, it spills out of the heart of one that realizes he is morally bankrupt. He prays as he does in this psalm not because of his goodness but in spite of his lack of it and because he has a firm grip on the character of the God who cares for moral failures, pardons their rebellious acts against Him, leads them back in the right way, and delivers them in the consequences their own wrongdoings have brought upon them.[62] David's path to God in this psalm can be yours. Follow him in his journey, and then make it your own.

GET DESPERATE BEFORE YOUR GOD

No flowery beginning adorns this psalm. From the opening salvo of its pithy first verse (only four words in Hebrew), David pants his need of deliverance: *To You, O Lord, I lift up my soul.* Desperation fuels his cry. This is not white-collar praying but rather the blue-collar kind that leaves you sweaty and drained when done. David is clearly in a difficult situation. His enemies are multiplying; embarrassment lurks around the corner (v. 2; cf. vv. 3, 19-20). He petitions to be delivered from both.

O my God, I trust in You; let me not be ashamed; let not my enemies triumph over me (v. 2).

Perhaps you also are facing embarrassment and multiplying enemies. Instability of character has left you with an erratic work history and angry former managers. Shameful past choices have now become public. Poor financial stewardship has you begging at the door of your relatives.

Get desperate. Remind Him who He is to you: *my God.* Let Him know that all your hopes of any deliverance are pinned on Him (as David does twice in vv. 2-3). Reiterate whose side you are on: you are not among those who are *wantonly treacherous* (v. 3; ESV). You have the privilege of crying out and expecting to be heard.

HUMBLY PLEAD FOR DIVINE GUIDANCE

Psalm 25 contains at least eight references to God's guidance. Only Psalm 119 contains more. David petitions God for direction and then expresses confidence of its receipt. Notice the guidance for which he prays:

*Make me to know **your** ways; teach me **your** paths. Lead me in **your** truth and teach me* (vv. 4-5).

David realizes that he needs God to keep him on *His* path. Straying from that path leads to the very kind of distressing circumstances that he is already contending with. Those who stay on the path experience unfailing love and faithfulness.

The LORD leads with unfailing love and faithfulness all who keep his covenant and obey his demands (v. 10; NLT).

Similarly, we can come to God for deliverance from our troubles—even when they are of our own making—when we are willing for God to guide us back to His path. Sin and its harsh consequences should produce submissiveness. God will teach sinners His way, but they must be meek sinners—those who confess the rightness of God's ways and desire His counsel.

Good and upright is the LORD; therefore He teaches sinners in the way. The **humble** *He guides in justice, and the* **humble** *He teaches His way … The secret of the LORD is with those who fear Him, and He will show them His covenant* (vv. 8-9, 14).

CONFESS YOUR SIN AND SEEK FORGIVENESS

Repeatedly in this psalm, David acknowledges his sinfulness and asks for forgiveness (vv. 6-7, 11, 18). Sins he committed as a young man flit before his mind. Acts of rebellion committed as an adult grieve him.

Do not remember the sins of my youth, nor my transgressions; according to Your mercy remember me, for Your goodness' sake, O LORD (v. 7).

Present guilt also weighs him down, either over some specific sin or because of an excited sensitivity to his innate depravity (v. 11). David realizes that reconciliation with God and pardon for sin must precede any hoped-for deliverance. His repentance when he sins is what sets him apart so utterly from his predecessor, King Saul, and from many other biblical characters. Even here in Psalm 25, David seeks neither to justify his sins nor to minimize them. He, in fact, paints himself quite black.

For your name's sake, O Lord, pardon my guilt, for **it is great** (v. 11).

In dealing with my children, I have noticed how proficient they are in minimizing their sin. They are not angry at a sibling, just frustrated. They did not kick their brother; they just stuck their foot in his direction. They did not hit their sister; they just tapped her. (How she bruised so easily remains inexplicable!) They were not tackling each other—just hugging each other down to the ground. I have heard statements like, "I accidentally hit him with a stick." Or, one of my personal favorites, "I shoved him out of the room because I know the Bible says to run from temptation; and if he stayed in the room, I was going to get mad and hurt him." My children are very spiritual sinners!

Truth be told, kids have nothing on adults. Our lies become creative explanations—partial truths, fudged a little, to be sure, but motivated (we assure ourselves) by altruistic considerations. Anger is retitled as irritation. Even apologies become didactic moments to point out our spouse's failures: "I am sorry for getting irritated when you did not launder my shirt on time" or "I am sorry that your laziness makes me lose my temper."

David's prayer, when it comes to his sin, is for God to forgive him (vv. 11, 18). He acknowledges that he has acted inappropriately toward God and deserves wrath; the pardon he seeks is completely undeserved. He recognizes that no man can take away the guilt of his own wrongdoing; God must lift it from him or it will stay with him always.[63] David's confession of sin gives us a pattern to follow when we have similarly failed our Lord.

EXPRESS YOUR CONFIDENCE IN GOD'S UNDESERVED HELP

Only one plea for forgiveness interrupts the otherwise unbroken sequence of confidence in God that marks the middle of the psalm (vv. 8-15). Even in the midst of trouble (which will come to the forefront at the end of the psalm) David finds his footing in the character of his God. Yes, he is a sinner, but he is also a humble God-fearer who seeks to keep God's covenant requirements. He can bank on God's guidance, goodness, uprightness, and blessing. What's more, he has an intimacy of access to the Lord, as if he is privy to confidential information (v. 14).

Remarkably, he remains confident in spite of the knowledge that his sins are so great (v. 11). Amid potentially embarrassing and ruinous circumstances, caused perhaps by his own sin, David still maintains his confidence that God will help him find the way out. He has learned a lesson that all of us could benefit from: God is our only hope of deliverance, even when our own sin might be behind our troubles.

David illustrates this beautifully in Psalm 3. He is on the run from his son Absalom, a consequence of his sin with Bathsheba. Enemies are multiplying against him—Absalom seemingly holds sway over the entire kingdom. Nevertheless, David cries to God for help and receives it (v. 4).

Jonah experienced God's help even when his dilemma was entirely one of his own making. Pinpointed by pagan sailors as the cause of the storm, Jonah still refused to repent, choosing to be thrown overboard rather than submit to God's decree for him to preach to the Ninevites. (Arguably, God would have stilled the storm immediately, if Jonah would have repented and agreed to preach at Nineveh.)

The cold splash woke him up to his immediate peril. He hit the water, started to go under, and began to pray. God's merciful answer was in the form of a fish. Jonah deserved nothing but a watery grave; God gave him a second chance.

Psalm 25 emboldens us to come to the very God we have offended and ask confidently for His help because of the forgiveness His character makes possible. He can be trusted to manage the damage our own actions have brought upon ourselves.

We are not talking here of a convenient escape out of all sin's deserved repercussions. No one ever gets away with any sin, and some consequences are bigger than others. We can remain confident, though, that God will help us in the midst of whatever chastisement He deems necessary. David, after sinfully numbering his armies and incurring divine displeasure, felt that way and told the prophet Gad, *I am in great distress. Let us fall into the hand of the LORD, for his mercy is great; but let me not fall into the hand of man* (2 Sam. 24:14).

Taking David's example as a pattern for us, we can plead the consequences of our sins before the Lord and cast ourselves upon His mercies.

David concludes this middle section of Psalm 25 (vv. 8-15) by turning again to his problems. He has assured himself of God's favor and friendship (vv. 8-14). He can now face his challenges with confidence knowing that God is the only one who can extricate him from the troubles that threaten him.

My eyes are continually toward the LORD, For He is the only One who will free my feet out of the net (v. 15; my translation).

SPECIFICALLY ASK GOD'S HELP WITH YOUR TROUBLES

David's cry for help, his humble entreaty for divine direction, his confession of his sin, and his confidence in God have not removed his troubles, but they have given him a platform from which to now cry out for more specific help. In verses 16-21, he itemizes his troubles. He has turned his eyes to Yahweh for help (v. 15); he now asks Yahweh to turn His eyes upon him and his troubles. *Turn Yourself to me* (v. 16) is literally "face me." Twice, he calls on the Lord to *look upon* his troubles and his enemies (vv. 18-19). He feels his troubles—he is lonely and afflicted. His troubles actually grow, not just the external multiplying of his enemies (v. 19), but the troubles that all of this has caused him internally: *the troubles of my heart have enlarged* (v. 17). Verses 20-21 end with similar themes to that with which the psalm began: requests to be delivered from enemies and embarrassment mingle with expressions of trust.

In the midst of enumerating his troubles, David once again thinks of his sins: *Consider my affliction and my trouble, and forgive all my sins* (v. 18). He stops short of saying sin caused his troubles, but there obviously exists in his mind a link of some kind. Again, we learn a valuable lesson from David: sin should not keep us from bringing our troubles to the Lord; rather, we must be sure to bring both to the Lord, ever mindful of the "intimate connection between suffering and sin."[64]

We do not know whether any specific sin of David's prompted the writing of Psalm 25. However, our knowledge of his life from other parts of Scripture reveals that David certainly knew what it was to reap the harsh consequences of his own sinful actions. Uzza's death due to David's failure to follow carefully God's prescribed directions for moving the Ark of the Covenant must have been deeply mortifying (1 Chron. 13:9-10; 15:13). David's sin with Bathsheba and the timing of her husband's early demise must have become choice palace gossip (even before the days of Facebook). David's enemies multiplied as a direct consequence of his sin of adultery, including among their number his son Absalom whose insurrection nearly cost David his kingdom. David's sin of numbering the army led to the death of 70,000 people (2 Sam. 24:15). Surely that did not help his political publicity ratings!

The point here is that David knows whereof he speaks when he connects trouble with sin. David committed some great sins against the Lord and received some severe spankings. However, Psalm 25 provides us with the encouragement that sinners—repentant ones, that is—should still call out to God for help in the midst of their crises, even if related in some way to sins they have committed.

Our natural human response lies in the opposite direction. Typically, when we have failed and are facing the consequences of our own sin, we know we are to blame and assume we must extract ourselves from our self-inflicted woes. We think that God will not help us, since what we are experiencing is our own fault. We forget how repentance unlocks the door of God's mercy.

I once had a student who was failing my class. He was already beyond the limit of allowed absences, and he had neglected to accomplish the class's basic requirements. I called him in for a conference, and we talked. In mercy I worked out a plan whereby he could still pass the class if he did not incur any more absences and if he completed some of his back assignments. I felt proud of myself for being such a kind teacher and making a way for him to succeed. To my astonishment, he was absent the next class. I could not believe it. I had made a plan for him to pass the class, but he was throwing my merciful actions right back in my face. Eventually, I had the chance to talk with him again and ask him why. He answered that he was embarrassed about his lapses in the class and, therefore, had decided that he would punish himself by making himself fail. This (he asserted) would make him more academically and spiritually disciplined in the future.

His self-flagellation epitomizes human nature. We somehow think that we are more spiritual if we punish ourselves. Do such actions really please God? Or do they mirror the disingenuous repentance of Judas Iscariot who tragically punished himself by taking his own life? (Even the Greek word for repentance used in Matthew 27:3 is different from the normal one.)

MY EMBARRASSING MISTAKE

Psalm 25 first became my friend after an embarrassing impulse-buy a few years ago. We were in the Philippines at the time, and two of my wife's sisters were in South Korea. I knew she would enjoy traveling there to see them and, frankly, any excuse to travel is good enough for me. So I purchased round-trip airline tickets to Seoul and back for our whole family. It was a snap decision—it had to be in order to get the ridiculously low fare that the discount airline was offering. However, there was one problem. One of the sisters we were going to see, whose husband was stationed at a military base near Seoul, was recalled back to the United States before the proposed date of our visit. Our trip had to be called off.

Frustrated, embarrassed, and feeling guilty (for wasting Kingdom money), I found consolation in Psalm 25. David's prayers for God's guidance, mercy, forgiveness, and deliverance met the felt-needs of my own troubled spirit!

Turn Yourself to me, and have mercy on me, for I am desolate and afflicted. The troubles of my heart have enlarged; bring me out of my distresses (vv. 16-17).

I called Cebu Pacific, our airline carrier. Amazingly, 85% of what I had spent was refunded to me. Enough of a return to be a comfort; enough of a loss to be a reminder against future hastiness.

Conclusion—
Working Toward a Decision

Work out your own salvation with fear and trembling (Phil. 2:12)

Planning your life God's way is the fruit of daily, weekly, monthly, and yearly decisions, and the cumulative impact of all those decisions on the trajectory of your life. One unwise choice may not sink your whole life in that instant, just as one nudge of the ship's helm in the wrong direction will not immediately cast it on the shoals, but if no corrective measures are taken, it can still spell disaster. In addition, one wrong decision often leads to another and before we know it, we may find ourselves cast upon a reef and broken up into a state of disrepair.

Because we understand the importance of making right decisions, we often want to mechanize the decision-making process. However, making decisions that please the Lord is not an automated twelve-step plan; it is a skill that any believer can (and must) develop. It is a skill you hone as you prayerfully apply God's Word to your unique circumstances over the course of your life. This yields another reason that learning to make biblically sound decisions is important: each decision betters your skill in making the next one.

This book is intended to equip you to improve your skill at making biblically-based, Christ-honoring decisions. As we wind our way to a conclusion, I thought it might be helpful to review, in summary fashion, some of the key thoughts we made along the way and to simplify, if possible, the decision-making process.

The place to begin is with your relationship to Jesus Christ. Until you bow before Him as Son of God and let Him take the helm of your life, there is no way that you will get your mission in life right. Flowing right out of this is the realization that to make the most of your time on planet earth you must apply God's Word to your life until it challenges (and changes) your thinking and behavior. Linked to this is the surrender of your body and your mind to the Lord. Without your full allegiance settled, you will not have the discernment needed to assess properly the circumstances, relationships, goals, and activities in your life. A good way to test your loyalty is to examine your life in light of the fundamentals of the revealed will of God—the virtues and actions that God has explicitly decreed (chapter five). If you are not making headway on those, it is unlikely that you are loyal enough to God to make right decisions about more specific matters. Your worldly astigmatism will distort your application of God's Word.

Once you have these preliminary matters squared away, you are ready to tackle whatever decision that lies before you. Assess your decision from three angles. Think of it as the **Triangle of Decision**.

FIRST ANGLE—WHAT DOES GOD SAY?

First of all, and most importantly, evaluate your decision from the angle of what **God** says about your situation. Pray earnestly and expectantly for wisdom; then, put feet to your prayers by shining the light of God's Word on your deliberations. Examine your decision in the light of Scriptural commands, relevant passages, biblical characters, general principles, and what God is teaching you in your personal devotions. You may need to seek advice from a godly believer in order to complete your collection of applicable passages. Leave no stone unturned in being thorough. The Bible is God's mouth, and you want to put it up to your ear for a good, long listen. Meditate on the passages you find until the Holy Spirit makes needed application of those words to your unique set of circumstances. If your decision is a type of open door, evaluate it biblically on the basis of our fourfold open-door test (see chapter ten): 1) What is the spiritual condition of the person opening the door? 2) What are your motives and goals for going through this open door? 3) What might be the consequences down the road? and 4) How do your spiritual advisors feel about the open door?

SECOND ANGLE—WHAT DO OTHERS SAY?

The second angle to consider is what **others**—godly others, in particular—think about your decision. Talk to wise counselors or seek help from those knowledgeable of you and/or your area of decision. Consider strongly the spiritual advice of the godly people in your life. When we pray for wisdom, we are implicitly asking God for the right information in order to make a wise decision, and that information will often come from other people or resources. Be humble enough to admit you are not an expert. Diligently research and gather data. Profit from those with secular expertise in a given field. Build a runway of appropriate length for the decision at hand.

THIRD ANGLE—WHO ARE YOU?

The third angle from which to assess your decision is in light of who **you** are: your God-given CV. How will your decision affect the strategic intersection of your uniqueness and God's kingdom? Your decision should continue the connect-the-dots picture that God is constructing your life to be. Avoid anything that will fling your life into a wild tangent. Be sure you are not making your decision out of a sense of discontentment over who you are or out of a desire to live out somebody else's story. As a believer delighting in the Lord, frankly ask yourself, "What do I want to do?" Your desire—especially a burden to contribute to God's kingdom in some specific way—is often the starting point for God's direction and may have been placed on your heart by God Himself.

Take the results of your **triangle**—what does **God** say? What input have **others** given? Who are **you**?—and lay them out before the Lord in prayer. If married, talk through them prayerfully with your spouse. Before you lay them out in prayer, it may help you to jot down key thoughts on a sheet of paper or into a computer spreadsheet so you can visually weigh the merits and minuses of your decision. If you are still radically unsure, work back through chapter twelve ("What to do when you are not sure what to do").

Then, make a decision and plan out its execution. Follow the plan of attack laid out in chapter eight ("Putting feet to your prayers for wisdom"). Since no one foresees his or her pathway perfectly, remain submitted to any God-given redirection to your plans. Do not brace yourself against divine redirection; rather, rejoice in it as a singular evidence of God's love, omniscience, and omnipotence.

I have found that when I have worked through a decision in this manner (whether in part or in whole), my genuine options narrow down to one or two. Generally, through prayer, further meditation over applicable Scripture, reviewing my research, and additional counsel, one option will detach itself from the rest and commend itself above all the others.

As you make your decision, do not forget that decision-making is a two-sided activity. As you work out your salvation [your life as a Christian] with fear and trembling, God is at work in you *to make you desire and do those things that bring Him pleasure* (Phil. 2:13; my paraphrase). Even the options that are available to you as you make a decision are of Him. Sometimes we erroneously think that we have to exhaustively check all our options from Boston to San Diego before we can make a sound decision—as if, for example, a man has to interview the three-plus billion girls on planet earth before coming to a decision on which one he should marry.

Yes, you must hone your skills at making decisions that please God. He wants you to! At the same time, trust the sovereignty of God in where He has placed you, the Scripture the Holy Spirit is illuminating to you, the counselors and resources He is providing, and the way He is connecting the dots in your life. He has a vested interest in you because you are in His Son. He is working everything together for good for those who love Him so that someday they will be like Christ, and He (Christ) will be the first among many brethren (Rom. 8:28-30). God's love for His Son and His resolve to glorify Him guarantees it.

Practical Help for Life Planning

LORD, make me to know my end, and what is the measure of my days (Psa. 39:4)

Now that you have read this book, are you any closer to planning your life God's way? You will close this book and re-enter a world full of pressures that pull you in multiple directions at the same time. What can you do immediately so that the biblical help you have gained in this book does not slip away unused?

Based on the principles outlined in this book, begin immediately by establishing your biblical priorities. These priorities are typically defined by your relationships or positions. For example, above everything else you are a child of God. Enhancing your relationship as a child of God is one of your biblical priorities. Are you a mother? A father? A daughter? A wife? A husband? Consider biblically your priorities in each of these spheres of your life. What else are you? You are a neighbor. You are a citizen. Do you have a job or a business? These also are part of your biblical priorities. Determine biblically what your priorities should be for each of these areas of your life. (Remember how we shine the light of God's Word on our pathway?)

My suggestion is that you identify four to five of your top relationships and then write down two or three biblical priorities for each.

Once you have identified your biblical priorities based on God's Word, then identify some goals to help you achieve those priorities. Goals should be attainable, measurable, and specific. For example, one of your biblical priorities as a child of God should be to grow in the grace and knowledge of your Lord and Savior, Jesus Christ. This assumes a daily time with Him. Now set a goal: "I will spend the first thirty minutes of every day in fellowship with Him." Maybe your goal should be much higher: "I will spend at least one hour in prayer every day." Or more specific: "I will read through the entire Bible this year and daily write down one truth about God that I will meditate on throughout that day."

Maybe as a wife you realize that one of your biblical priorities is your husband and that God wants you to reverence him. Turn that into a goal: "I will say one respectful thing to my husband every day."

Again, I would recommend that you limit your goals per relationship to two or three. Keep it simple. Keep it achievable.

Even within the limitations I am suggesting, you will find it overwhelming to juggle all of your responsibilities. Welcome to being an adult! An adult goes to bed every night with most of the goals on his or her to-do list unfinished. So how can you accomplish those goals? You are probably already predicting the feeling of guilt that will gnaw away at you when you crash and burn. In fact, you know you will fail: so why even try?

I recommend that you make some kind of a daily or weekly schedule. You have established your biblical priorities, and you have thought through goals to accomplish those priorities. Now, to accomplish those goals you need to make a plan as to how you will actually use your time. For example, if you chose as one of your goals to spend the first thirty minutes of your day in fellowship with God, you need to log that activity on your daily or weekly schedule in order to make it happen. Mentally work through your morning routine to determine what time you will need to wake up in order to accomplish your Bible-reading goal. That, in turn, may necessitate going to bed a little earlier at night.

Start your time budget by plotting those things that are non-negotiable or are decided for you: three meals a day, church attendance, hours in the office, etc. Then begin logging activities on your weekly schedule in order of your biblical priorities. Being a child of God is number one, so write in first that precious time with your Savior. Times of rest or re-creation are necessary; plan those in your schedule too. Then continue from there. Don't be afraid to make adjustments to your schedule as you go along. Fine-tuning your schedule is not a sign of failure but rather a symptom of growth.

Once you have made your time budget based on your biblical priorities, live by it. Obviously things will happen that will throw you off schedule. That's okay. That's part of being human. Pick back up tomorrow where you left off today. What will console you is the knowledge that you are using your days to work your biblical priorities. Yes, you will go to bed with things unfinished. On the other hand, you will have the confidence of knowing that you have used your time wisely. You will also find that you get more done in a day because you have specific goals and clear-cut time allotted to accomplish them.

For example, let's consider the issue of email and social media. Too often, we allow our culture's social media expectations to consume exorbitant quantities of our time. (For some inexplicable reason, we receive absurd fulfillment in wasting time on these matters.) Then afterwards we feel guilty or even stressed because more crucial things did not get done. Solve that by allotting a specific time in your day to email. When you allot only thirty minutes a day—say, 1:00-1:30 pm—to answer email, update Facebook and whatever social media applications you maintain, you will find out how much you can get done in thirty minutes. Surprisingly, you may find that you did not need two hours; you were just dawdling. Now you have ninety minutes of extra time to throw at your biblical priorities. Number your days (your time) and apply your heart to that which is truly wise (Psa. 90:12).

Charles Simeon, pastor of Holy Trinity Church in Cambridge from 1782 until his death in 1836, hung in his dining room a portrait of Henry Martyn, the pioneer missionary to India whose unremitting labors contributed to his early decease at the age of only thirty-one. The picture constantly reminded Simeon not to trifle. We all would do well to make a screen saver of the most diligent person we know so that his or her face will haunt us in those moments that we squander. What do you want to be known for or remembered as? Think about that on every occasion you choose to fritter away your time.

If you are still not convinced about the value of making a weekly/daily time schedule, then do this: live without it for another week and keep track, instead, of what you actually do with your time. You will look back and be amazed at how much time you wasted during the week. No wonder you are not fulfilling your biblical priorities! It is not because you do not have the time—we all have the same amount of time. It is because you are not wisely using the time you have. People who accomplish great things for God are not people who have more time; they are people who make the most of the time they have.

Many believers stay up way too late at night piddling on the internet, watching movies, or flipping from one television news channel to another. Then they wake up too tired the next day to achieve their goals. (Remember that goal of thirty minutes with the Lord every morning?) Take control of those evening hours. Even secular experts are recommending no screen time sixty to ninety minutes before bed. Why? Electronic gadgets stimulate the body and affect the quality of one's sleep. Plus, when you are tired, you are tempted to watch whatever the world throws your way on the TV or the internet. You will then feel guilty because you know that you have not carefully guarded your eyes and heart or used that time advantageously. Leverage your time by going to bed earlier so you can wake up and spend quality time with the Lord.

Again, take control by making a plan of how you will use your time. Plan your rest. Plan your recreation. Want to have a game night with your family? Plan it. Retain control over it! Want to check the news? Plan the right time of the day for that and keep it within God-honoring limitations.

You have only one life, and that life is very short. Time methodically and irreplaceably ticks away your mortality. You have one chance to make a difference for God's kingdom. One chance to get your mission right. One chance to live your life God's way. One chance on earth to glorify God. Your life is composed of time. How much time? Nobody knows! That's why time—not your money, not your possessions—is your greatest commodity. Just watch people caught in the grip of a fatal disease. They will gladly expend all their money just to buy a little more time.

So don't waste your precious time. Most of us are very careful with our money. We will do anything to save a buck, and then we will boastfully post on Facebook our proud accomplishment. But how often do we squander time? You can always make more money, but you cannot make more time. Do you have a doctor's appointment? Bring along a book that you planned to finish this year. Caught in car-line after school? Use that time to memorize verses, encourage another waiting parent, or cross-stitch. Do something constructive, even if it is mastering a kazoo or developing your origami skills!

Rejoice in your God as you plan out your days and hours. Enjoy your life. Enjoy your priorities. Enjoy your goals. Enjoy your plan as you work it. Enjoy today. "Open the windows and drink in the day." By living according to a daily/weekly schedule, you will enjoy your life because you will know that you are spending it wisely. Your life will truly be *blessed*, in the best and biblical sense of the word, achieving a happiness envied by others and honoring to your Lord, because you are planning your life and living it God's way.

About the Author

Timothy W. Berrey is the Director of Graduate Studies at Bob Jones Memorial Bible College in Manila, Philippines. In addition to teaching both undergraduate and graduate courses, he also oversees the Continuing Education for Pastors program, an extended education program for pastors that is held in various locations in the Philippines for the purpose of enabling men who are currently pastoring in the province to attain a seminary-level education. He regularly teaches and ministers in other countries across Asia, as well as serving as an adjunct professor at Baptist College of Ministry in Wisconsin. Prior to becoming a full-time missionary with Gospel Fellowship Association, he was active in his local church ministry as well as teaching and pastoring in missions endeavors in Africa, Europe, and Asia. Timothy holds a Ph.D. in Old Testament Interpretation from Bob Jones University in Greenville, South Carolina.

For more information, visit Livewithamission.com.

Also by Timothy W. Berrey

From Eden to Patmos: An Overview of Biblical History will guide you on a fascinating journey through the timeline of Scripture with a fresh approach that makes biblical chronology accessible for nearly anyone wishing to deepen their faith through a greater understanding of history.

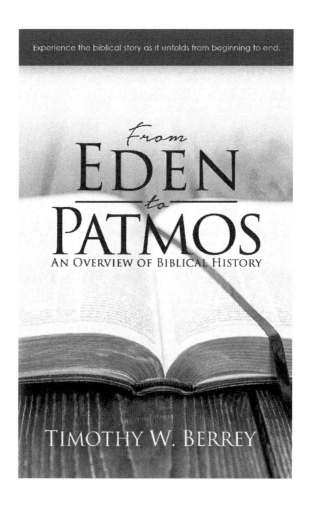

Notes

Notes

1 Some say he learned twenty-six languages; others say, forty-five. My guess is that he learned twenty-six up through his planned language-learning years but continued to dabble at languages throughout his life, until the number reached forty-five. An excellent summary of his life is written by Brian Nicks, "The Life and Work of Robert Dick Wilson," *The Master's Seminary Journal,* Volume 19, Issue 1 (Spring 2008), pp. 91-106.

2 The Old Testament word *blessed* (*'ašrê*) is one of "envious desire." *Theological Wordbook of the Old Testament*, ed. R. Laird Harris, Gleason L. Archer Jr., and Bruce K. Waltke (Moody, 1999), p. 80.

3 From www.nytimes.com/1995/09/17/us/doctor-who-cut-off-wrong-leg-is-defended-by-colleagues.html, accessed on October 5, 2016.

4 Those of you with a keen philosophical bent will have to forgive me for starting here. I realize that there are questions arguably more fundamental and logically prior.

5 See *monogenes* in William Arndt, Frederick W. Danker, and Walter Bauer, *A Greek-English Lexicon of the New Testament and Other Early Christian Literature* (University of Chicago Press, 2000), p. 658; hereafter, abbreviated as BDAG.

6 Luke 3:38 refers to Adam as "the son of God," but the actual Greek word for son does not occur in the text (note the italics in the KJV and NKJV).

7 Consult, for example, Robert M. Bowman Jr. and J. Ed Komoszewski, *Putting Jesus in His Place: The Case for the Deity of Christ* (Kregel Publications, 2007).

8 Actually, to be technical, this Voice would prepare the way for the **Lord**, yet another affirmation of the deity of Jesus. See also Malachi 3:1.

9 Ravi Zacharias, *Jesus Among Other Gods* (W Publishing, 2000), pp. 37-38.

10 Max Lucado, *Cure for the Common Life: Living in Your Sweet Spot* (Thomas Nelson, 2008), p. 13.

11 Os Guiness, *The Call: Finding and Fulfilling the Central Purpose of Your Life* (Thomas Nelson, 2003), p. 47.

12 Lucado, p. 7.

13 Guiness reminds us that "the purpose of giftedness is stewardship and service, not selfishness" (p. 45).

14 Rodolfo Salas, *Prioritize 'til It Hurts: Discovering and Unleashing Your Best Opportunities* (University Press, 2003).

15 Gerald Sittser, *The Will of God as a Way of Life: How to Make Every Decision with Peace and Confidence,* rev. ed. (Zondervan, 2004), p. 46.

[16] Vishal and Ruth Mangalwadi, *The Legacy of William Carey: A Model for the Transformation of a Culture* (Crossway Books, 1999), p. 134.

[17] Bruce K. Waltke with Cathi J. Fredricks, *Genesis: A Commentary* (Zondervan, 2001), p. 155.

[18] Harold W. Hoehner, *Ephesians: An Exegetical Commentary* (Baker Academic, 2002), p. 691.

[19] See *suniemi* in BDAG, p. 972.

[20] Willem A. VanGemeren, "Psalms," in vol. 5 of *The Expositor's Bible Commentary: Psalms, Proverbs, Ecclesiastes, Song of Songs*, ed. Frank E. Gaebelein (Zondervan, 1991), p. 228.

[21] BDAG, p. 995 (*teleios*).

[22] Robert H. Mounce, *Romans,* vol. 27 in the New American Commentary (Broadman & Holman, 1995), p. 233.

[23] William Hendriksen, *Exposition of Paul's Epistle to the Romans,* New Testament Commentary (Baker, 1980-1981), p. 406.

[24] Gordon T. Smith, in *How Then Should We Choose: Three Views on God's Will and Decision Making,* ed. Douglas S. Huffman (Kregel Publications, 2009), Kindle Ed., Loc. 2392.

[25] James Denney, "St Paul's Epistle to the Romans," in vol. 2 of *The Expositor's Greek Testament* (George H. Doran Company, n.d.), p. 688.

[26] Revelation 22:17 helps to maintain the balance: We wished to drink of the water of life, and we did so!

[27] The Greek word, translated *moderation* in the NKJV, means self-control and suggests prudence or good judgment.

[28] BDAG, p. 982, proposes *thrive* and *prosper* as valid glosses for the passive of the verb "to save" (*sozo*).

[29] Paul Hattaway, *Back to Jerusalem: Three Chinese House Church Leaders Share Their Vision to Complete the Great Commission* (IVP Books, 2005), pp. 82-83.

[30] This observation is found in Emerson Eggerichs, *Love and Respect: The Love She Most Desires, The Respect He Desperately Needs* (Integrity Publishers, 2004), p. 250, but it is not original with them.

[31] J. B. Williams, *Memoirs of the Life, Character, and Writings of the Rev. Matthew Henry* (Peirce & Williams, 1830), p. 241. A widely quoted fourfold giving of thanks by Henry—"I thank Thee first because I was never robbed before; second, because although they took my purse they did not take my life; third, because although they took my all, it was not much; and fourth because it was I who was robbed, and not I who robbed"—is apparently a misquote (unless Henry alludes to this event again in other unpublished writings of his).

[32] Kevin DeYoung, *Just Do Something: A Liberating Approach to Finding God's Will* (Moody, 2009), p. 24.

[33] A form of this quote is often attributed to Winston Churchill, but it probably does not originate with him.

[34] Arnold A. Dallimore, vol. 1 of *George Whitefield: The Life and Times of the Great Evangelist of the Eighteenth-Century Revival* (Banner of Truth, 1970), p. 273.

[35] Narrated by DeYoung, pp. 82-83.

[36] Henry and Richard Blackaby in *How Then Should We Choose* (Kindle Ed., Loc. 287) actually use this verse as an example of a passage from which New Testament Christians can still legitimately draw comfort. I would agree as long as we draw a principle that is truly timeless rather than claiming it as a specific promise for ourselves.

[37] This story comes from the recollections of a certain James P. Smith, inserted by Mary Anna Jackson in her *Life and Letters of General Thomas J. Jackson (Stonewall Jackson)* [Harper & Brothers, 1892], p. 394.

[38] Sinclair B. Ferguson, *From the Mouth of God: Trusting, Reading, and Applying the Bible* (Banner of Truth Trust, 2014), p. ix.

[39] DeYoung, p. 67, points this out.

[40] His leadership transforms our speech, for example: in almost every case where Spirit filling occurs, the result affects the speech of the person involved (Luke 1:42, 67; 10:21; Acts 2:4, 17; 4:8, 31; 7:55; Eph. 5:18-21).

[41] Nehemiah's admission, "Then my God put it into my heart" (Neh. 7:5), may have some relevance to this discussion.

[42] "God is not in a box, and as a result he can (and from time to time does) reveal his will to individuals in special ways. There are too many Christians who rightly attest to such leading to deny it." James Montgomery Boice, *Romans: The Reign of Grace*, vol. 2 (Baker Book House, 1992), p. 888.

[43] Hoehner, p. 211.

[44] I am indebted in my wording to Peter T. O'Brien, *Colossians, Philemon*, vol. 44, Word Biblical Commentary (Word, 1998), p. 20. Here's the way he says it: "The content [*ina*] of the petition is that God (the passive [*plerothete*] shows it is he who supplies this knowledge in abundance) might fill the Colossian Christians with a perception of his will, which consists of an understanding of what is spiritually important."

[45] J. I. Packer, *Hot Tub Religion* (Tyndale House, 1987), p. 91.

[46] "Let him ask" is a third person imperative in Greek.

[47] I am borrowing these words from John Eliot (1604-1690), missionary to the Algonquian Indians. Quoted more fully (from the last page of his Indian grammar), his words are as follows: "We must not sit still, and look for miracles; Up and be doing, and the Lord will be with thee. Prayer and Pains, through Faith in Christ Jesus, will do anything." *The Indian Grammar Begun* (Cambridge: Marmaduke Johnson, 1666), p. 66.

[48] *Imitation of Christ*, p. 34.

[49] Missionary Joel James deserves the credit for calling my attention to this passage's relevancy for assessing open doors. See his booklet titled *Biblical Decision-Making: Is It God's Will to "Find" His will?*, pp. 24-26, accessible as of

October 9, 2016, at http://gracefellowship.co.za/wp-content/uploads/2015/10/James_Joel-Decision-making.pdf. James makes some helpful observations, although I do not agree with all of his conclusions.

[50] Derek Kidner observes, "its [the King of Sodom's offer] sole disadvantage is perceptible, again, only to faith....The struggle of kings, the far-ranging armies and the spoil of a city are the small-change of the story; the crux is the faith or failure of one man." *Genesis: An Introduction and Commentary* (InterVarsity Press, 1967), p. 132.

[51] Guiness, p. 28. A very good biography of Wilberforce, for those interested, is Eric Metaxas' *Amazing Grace: William Wilberforce and the Heroic Campaign to End Slavery* (HarperOne, 2007).

[52] Attributed to German poet and translator Karl von Knebel (1744-1834).

[53] Ishmael was "of the seed royal," meaning that he was a descendant of David (2 Kings 25:25).

[54] Albert W. Lorimer, *God Runs My Business: The Story of R. G. LeTourneau* (Fleming H. Revell Company, 1941), p. 41

[55] Sittser, pp. 85ff.

[56] Ibid., pp. 90, 93.

[57] Lucado, p. 7.

[58] Boice, p. 885. His extended discussion, which continues through p. 900, is quite helpful.

[59] John MacArthur Jr., *Found: God's Will* (David C. Cook Publishers, 2012), p. 94. Realize, though, that he says this after devoting over eighty percent of his book to a probing spiritual analysis of our commitment to obey.

[60] Ibid., pp. 68-69.

[61] Although it has a couple irregularities and v. 22 stands technically outside of the acrostic pattern.

[62] I am paraphrasing here a beautiful application about prayer that Goldingay draws from his study of Psalm 25. Here are his exact words: "Prayer acknowledges that we are moral failures but knows that Yhwh cares about people who fail in their commitment. It thus owns our need for Yhwh to put our failures and wrongdoing out of mind, to pardon these, and to carry them—deeds of long ago that we might not really be very responsible for, and deeds of our adulthood for which we have no excuse." John Goldingay, *Baker Commentary on the Old Testament: Psalms 1–41*, ed. Tremper Longman III, (Baker Academic, 2006), p. 378.

[63] *Pardon* (v. 11) "is the cancellation of the significance of a wrong act that Yhwh alone can effect." Ibid., p. 373.

[64] Joseph A. Alexander, *Commentary on Psalms* (Kregel Publications, 1991), p. 125.